Contents

MW01145621

Unit 1: Growth of Civilizations

Content Vocabulary: archaeology, artifact, cultivate, culture, domesticate, migration, nomad, prehistoric
Academic Vocabulary: differentiate, significance

Content Vocabulary: ancient, autocracy, bureaucracy, dynasty, empire, monotheism, pharaoh, polytheism
Academic Vocabulary: relevant, verify

Content Vocabulary: aristocracy, decline, democracy, dictator, ethics, philosophy, republic, rhetoric
Academic Vocabulary: paraphrase, predict

Unit 2: Growth of Nations

Content Vocabulary: chivalry, feudalism, heretic, hierarchy, manor, medieval, nobility, peasant
Academic Vocabulary: formulate, refute

Content Vocabulary: apprentice, barter, conquest, crusade, guild, plague, scholar, theocracy
Academic Vocabulary: react, rephrase

Content Vocabulary: commercial, commodity, compass, isolationism, mercantilism, navigation, renaissance, tariff
Academic Vocabulary: generalize, infer

Content Vocabulary: absolutism, despotism, diplomacy, monarchy, parliament, reign, restoration, sovereign
Academic Vocabulary: articulate, fallacy

Vocabulary: World History, SV 9781419035029

Contents, *continued*

Introduction

Building a strong academic and content vocabulary is the key to success in science and social studies. Current reading research indicates that vocabulary is the major factor in improving comprehension. Research also shows that students benefit from a multi-strategy approach that exposes students to vocabulary in a variety of contexts. *Vocabulary in the Content Areas* is designed to supplement basal content-area textbooks by providing theme-based vocabulary study aligned to best-selling science and social studies textbooks and standards-based assessments.

> "Students learn new words better when they encounter them often and in various contexts. The more children see, hear, and work with specific words, the better they seem to learn them."
>
> *Put Reading First* (2001)

What is *Vocabulary in the Content Areas*?
- A developmental, research-based, interactive program designed to help students build a strong vocabulary foundation in science and social studies

How does *Vocabulary in the Content Areas* build a strong vocabulary foundation?
- Through explicit instruction, practice, and application of both content-area and academic vocabulary

What are content-area vocabulary and academic vocabulary?
- Content-area vocabulary refers to the subject-specific words that students need to understand content-area concepts. Examples: *amphibian, cellular, democracy, inflation*
- Academic vocabulary refers to the words and phrases that facilitate academic discourse and that are used across several content areas. Examples: *suggest, illustrate, analyze, diagram*

What skills and strategies does *Vocabulary in the Content Areas* target to help students with their content-area coursework?
- building associations with word anchors
- using word study skills such as affixes and roots
- using parts of speech and multiple meanings
- using synonyms and antonyms and comparisons and contrasts
- using specific context clues such as in-text definitions, examples, and descriptions

In what contexts does *Vocabulary in the Content Areas* teach vocabulary?
- reading
- listening
- writing
- speaking
- test practice

In sum, *Vocabulary in the Content Areas* helps students develop a robust academic vocabulary that supports them in
- comprehension of content-area textbooks
- meaningful participation in class discussion of content-area concepts
- production of articulate content-area writing
- success on content-area, standards-based assessments

Vocabulary: World History, SV 9781419035029

Features

Vocabulary Strategy and Reading Passages

Students practice the focus strategy with two high-interest reading passages. Suggestions for note taking and marking key information in the text also help students prepare for reading passages on standardized tests.

New World History Words and Other Useful Words

Student-friendly definitions are provided for content-area and academic vocabulary.

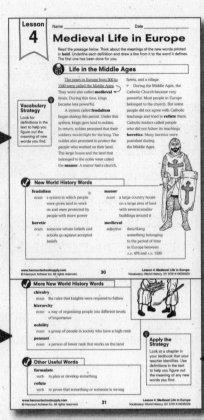

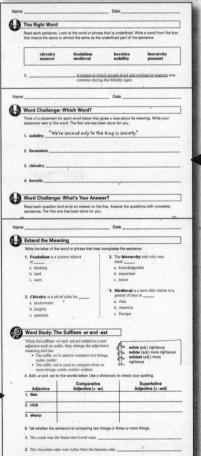

Apply the Strategy

Students practice the focus strategy with their content-area textbooks.

Vocabulary Practice

Students receive ample practice with content and vocabulary through multiple encounters with words in a variety of contexts.

Word Study

Students both deepen their understanding of lesson words and increase their vocabulary acquisition through explicit instruction and practice with root words and affixes.

Vocabulary: World History, SV 9781419035029

Features, *continued*

The Language of Testing

Students build confidence and master the language of tests through test-taking tips, strategies, and practice with the types of questions they will encounter on high-stakes tests.

*Answers for the multiple-choice questions in this section were included in the Answer Key for discussion purposes. It is up to teacher discretion to require students to answer the multiple-choice questions in this section.

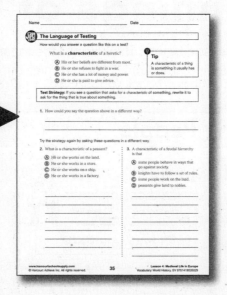

On Your Own

Students create their own understanding of content-area and academic vocabulary by answering questions that encourage thinking about the words in a variety of contexts.

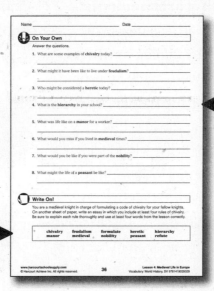

Write On!

A writing activity allows students to engage with the lesson vocabulary and concepts while also practicing key writing skills.

Assessment

Assessments for lessons provide an opportunity to monitor students' progress and give students practice answering questions in a standardized-test format.

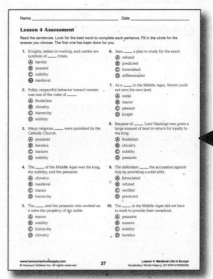

Vocabulary: World History, SV 9781419035029

Name _____ Date _____

Beginnings of Civilization

Read the passage below. Think about the meanings of the new words printed in **bold**. Underline any definitions that might help you figure out what these words mean. The first one has been done for you.

Early People

Vocabulary Strategy

Writers will often include definitions of new or difficult words near those words in a text. Look for definitions in the text to help you understand new words.

The first people lived thousands of years ago. They lived during **prehistoric** times, or the <u>period before people learned how to write their languages</u>. We have learned a lot about the way early people lived from the work of **archaeologists**. Archaeologists are scientists who study the past by finding **artifacts**, or objects that were made by people long ago. The **significance**, or importance, of artifacts is that they tell us how people lived long ago.

The first people lived in Africa. They lived in a world that had no stores and no electricity. These early people learned to hunt animals. They made clothing from animal skins. They also found plants, nuts, and berries that they ate to survive.

The first people were **nomads**, people who move from place to place. When they could no longer find food in one place, they moved to another. Wherever they lived, they always began a new search for food.

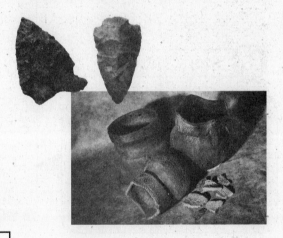

New World History Words

archaeology

noun the study of the buildings, tools, and way of life of people of the past

artifact

noun a tool or object that is made by and used by a person

nomad

noun a person who moves from place to place to find food

prehistoric

noun people and things that existed before history was written down

Now read this passage and practice the vocabulary strategy again. Underline any definitions in the passage that help you figure out what the new words in **bold** mean.

The Beginning of Village Life

It was difficult for early people to live as nomads. Life became easier when people learned to use fire. Fire helped them cook food and stay warm.

Life became easier when early people learned to **cultivate**, or grow, fruits and vegetables. They learned to **differentiate**, or tell the difference, between plants that were safe and those that contained poison. They also learned to **domesticate**, or tame, wild animals. They tamed pigs, dogs, horses, and goats. Some animals were used to help with farm work. Others were used for food.

As early people learned to farm, **migration**, or movement, took place from Africa to other places. People migrated to Asia, the Middle East, and other places. The early farmers learned to live and work together in villages. They developed **cultures**. A culture is the shared traditions and beliefs of a group of people. As time passed, some of these early cultures developed into civilizations. You will read more about early civilizations in Lesson 2.

 More New World History Words

cultivate
verb to prepare land to grow crops, or to develop something to make it better

culture
noun the shared traditions and beliefs of a group of people

domesticate
verb to tame animals and grow plants for human use

migration
noun movement from one region or country to another

How do you like being **domesticated**?

The work's hard, but I like the **culture**.

 Apply the Strategy

Look at a chapter in your textbook that your teacher identifies. Use definitions in the text to help you figure out the meaning of any new words you find.

 Other Useful Words

differentiate
verb to show the difference between things

significance
noun importance

Name _____   Date _____

Find the Word

Write a word from the box next to each clue. Then write the word formed by the boxed letters to finish the sentence below.

domesticate	**culture**	**migration**	**nomad**
archaeology	**artifact**	**prehistoric**	

1. movement from one region or country to another ___ ___ ___ [ ] ___ ___ ___ ___ ___

2. a group's shared traditions and beliefs ___ ___ ___ ___ ___ ___ [ ]

3. to tame animals ___ ___ [ ] ___ ___ ___ ___ ___ ___ ___

4. the study of past people [ ] ___ ___ ___ ___ ___ ___ ___ ___ ___

5. tool or object made and used by a person ___ ___ ___ [ ] ___ ___ ___ ___

6. someone who moves from place to place ___ ___ [ ] ___ ___ ___ ___

7. before history was written ___ ___ ___ ___ [ ] ___ ___ ___ ___ ___

Archaeologists study people of the past by looking at ___ ___ ___ ___ ___ ___ ___ ___ .

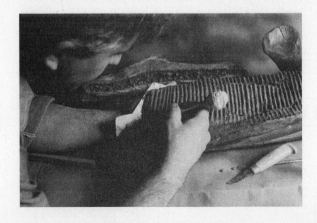

Name _____   Date _____

Word Challenge: Word Associations

Read the groups of words below. Write the word from the lesson that goes best with each group. The first one has been done for you.

1. _____artifact_____ a stone axe, clay bowls, arrowheads

2. _____ importance, value, meaning

3. _____ tame, control, train

4. _____ tell apart, separate, show differences

Word Challenge: Quick Pick

Read each question. Think of a response and write it on the line. Explain your answer. The first one has been done for you.

1. Which is an **artifact**: a plant or a stone axe? _A stone axe is an artifact_
   because a person made it.

2. Is a person who moves a lot a **nomad** or **prehistoric**? _____
   _____

3. If you wanted to train a dog, would you **domesticate** or **cultivate** it?
   _____

4. In **archaeology**, would you study an ancient pot or a modern map?
   _____

Vocabulary: World History, SV 9781419035029

Name _____   Date _____

Analogies

Use a word from the box to finish each sentence. Write the word on the line.

domesticate	nomad	archaeology	prehistoric

1. Artifacts are to _____ as rocks are to geology.

2. Tame is to _____ as act is to perform.

3. Govern is to politician as travel is to _____.

4. Ancient is to _____ as fit is to athletic.

Word Study: The Suffix -ation

When the suffix -ation is added to a verb such as migrate, it does two things:

- First, it changes the verb to a noun: migration.
- Second, it changes the word's meaning. The word now means "movement from one region or country to another."

Drop the -e from the end of a word before adding -ation.

migrate (v.) to move from one region or country to another
migration (n.) movement from one region or country to another

A. Add -ation to the following root words to make a new word and write a definition for each. Use a dictionary to check your spelling and your definitions.

	+ -ation	Definition
1. **cultivate**		
2. **domesticate**		
3. **examine**		

B. Write a new -ation word from above on each line.

1. The _____ of animals allows us to have pets.

2. The process of preparing land to grow crops is called _____.

Vocabulary: World History, SV 9781419035029

Name _____   Date _____

The Language of Testing

How would you answer a question like this on a test?

Identify a fact that tells you a group of people were prehistoric.

    Ⓐ They weren't very strong.
    Ⓑ They didn't use tools.
    Ⓒ They lived before people could write.
    Ⓓ They couldn't walk very far.

Tip

When you *identify*, you point out or name something. In a test question, the word *identify* means that you need to choose or pick the correct answer.

Test Strategy: Make sure you understand the question. Read it carefully. If you see a question that uses the word *identify*, rewrite it using the words *choose* or *pick*.

1. How could you say the question above in a different way?

_____

_____

Try the strategy again by asking these questions in a different way.

2. Identify the correct definition for the word *nomads*.

    Ⓐ people who move from place to place
    Ⓑ people who lived before history was written down
    Ⓒ people who study the past
    Ⓓ people who make objects or tools

_____

_____

_____

_____

3. Identify something that has to do with *migration*.

    Ⓐ creating a new set of beliefs
    Ⓑ growing new crops
    Ⓒ moving to a new country
    Ⓓ buying a new home

_____

_____

_____

_____

Lesson 1: Beginnings of Civilization
Vocabulary: World History, SV 9781419035029

Name _____ Date _____

 On Your Own

Answer the questions.

1. What subjects would you learn about if you studied **archaeology**? _____

_____

2. What can you learn from an **artifact**? _____

_____

3. What kind of things can you **cultivate**? _____

_____

4. What things do many **cultures** have in common? _____

_____

5. What animals have been **domesticated** by humans? _____

_____

6. What makes people and animals choose **migration** over staying someplace? _____

_____

7. How would you live if you were a **nomad**? _____

_____

8. What things could be described as **prehistoric**? _____

_____

 Write On!

You are an archaeologist who has discovered a special artifact. On another sheet of paper, write a short essay describing the artifact and explaining what it tells you about the people who used it. Use four or more words from the lesson correctly.

archaeology	artifact	culture	cultivate	differentiate
domesticate	migration	nomad	prehistoric	significance

Name _____   Date _____

Lesson 1 Assessment

Read the sentences. Look for the best word to complete each sentence. Fill in the circle for the answer you choose. The first one has been done for you.

1. The _____ of this key is that it is the only one that will allow us to open the lockbox.
   - (A) significance
   - (B) artifact
   - (C) migration
   - (D) culture

2. Blanca took classes in the _____ department so she could participate in digs in South America.
   - (A) culture
   - (B) archaeology
   - (C) nomads
   - (D) migration

3. Steven carefully _____ his garden by watering and weeding it regularly.
   - (A) domesticated
   - (B) cultivated
   - (C) differentiated
   - (D) migrated

4. The builders uncovered several _____ while digging the basement for a new house.
   - (A) artifacts
   - (B) cultures
   - (C) nomads
   - (D) significances

5. The Bering Land Bridge allowed nomads from Asia to _____ to North America.
   - (A) domesticate
   - (B) differentiate
   - (C) migrate
   - (D) significant

6. I cannot _____ between diet and regular soda.
   - (A) domesticate
   - (B) cultivate
   - (C) migrate
   - (D) differentiate

7. Dogs are the _____, or tame, species of a family that includes wolves, foxes, and coyotes.
   - (A) archaeological
   - (B) migrated
   - (C) domesticated
   - (D) differentiated

8. Most of what we have learned about _____ people has come from the study of artifacts.
   - (A) prehistoric
   - (B) cultivated
   - (C) significant
   - (D) domestic

9. Tribes of _____ moved from place to place in search of food.
   - (A) cultures
   - (B) migrations
   - (C) nomads
   - (D) artifacts

10. Jazz music is an important part of United States _____.
    - (A) artifacts
    - (B) culture
    - (C) archaeology
    - (D) migration

Lesson 2

Ancient Civilizations

Read the passage below. Decide if each new word in **bold** is a noun or verb. In the space above each new word, write *noun* or *verb*. Four of the new words in the passage are nouns. The first one has been done for you. Use this information with other clues in the text to figure out what each new word means.

Early People

Vocabulary Strategy

Identify if a new word is used as a noun, verb, adjective, or adverb to help you use other clues in the text to figure out the meaning of the new words.

About 7,000 years ago, the people of Egypt developed their own culture along the Nile River. Egypt is a hot dry country, but water from the Nile made it possible to farm the land.

noun Egypt's government was an **autocracy**. The **pharaoh**, or king, had total power to make laws. Egypt's government also had a large **bureaucracy**. In a bureaucracy, people do many different kinds of jobs for the government.

The people of Egypt practiced **polytheism**, which means that they believed in many gods. Their most important god was the sun god. They also believed the pharaoh was a god.

The Egyptians built huge pyramids as tombs for the pharaohs. These pyramids were in the shape of triangles. Thousands of slaves built each pyramid. The pyramids were built so well that they have lasted for thousands of years. The art and objects inside these pyramids **verify**, or prove, these facts about life along the Nile long ago.

New World History Words

autocracy

noun   a government controlled by one person who has total power

bureaucracy

noun   all of the rules followed by a government department, or a system in which many people in many jobs help run the government

pharaoh

noun   a king in ancient Egypt

polytheism

noun   belief in more than one god

Name _____ Date _____

Now read the passage below and practice the vocabulary strategy again. Write *noun, verb,* or *adjective* above each new word.

Other Ancient Civilizations

Civilizations developed in many parts of the world. These **ancient**, or old, civilizations had art, music, religion, cities, and governments. Most ancient people prayed to many gods. The Jews, however, were one group of people that believed in only one god. A belief in one god is called **monotheism**. The Jews also believed that their god wanted people to be honest and kind. Jews lived in the land that is now called Israel.

The ancient Persians conquered other countries and built a large **empire**. An empire is made up of a number of countries that have one ruler. Every part of the huge Persian empire had to obey the same laws.

Another great civilization developed in China. China was ruled by **dynasties**. A dynasty is a family of rulers. Sometimes the same dynasty ruled China for hundreds of years. The Chinese created beautiful art and cloth. They also spread important ideas. However, another **relevant**, or important, fact about Chinese culture is their respect for family life. Children learned to respect their parents and grandparents at an early age. Respect for parents and grandparents continues to be important in China today.

 More New World History Words

ancient
   adjective   belonging to the distant past

dynasty
   noun   a ruling family

empire
   noun   a number of countries that are all under the control of one ruling country

monotheism
   noun   a belief in one god

The family's an **autocracy**!

No, we're more of a **bureaucracy**. We all have jobs to do, and yours is to take out the trash.

 Apply the Strategy

Look at a chapter in your textbook that your teacher identifies. Identify parts of speech to help you figure out the meaning of any new words you find.

 Other Useful Words

relevant
   adjective   relating to something

verify
   verb   using evidence to check if something is true

Name _____ Date _____

Finish the Sentence

Use a word from the box to finish each sentence. Write the correct word on the line.

ancient	autocracy	bureaucracy	dynasties
empire	monotheism	pharaohs	polytheism

1. Ancient China was ruled by _____, or families of rulers.

2. The pyramids of ancient Egypt were built for the _____.

3. The Middle East was home to many _____ civilizations that were started thousands of years ago.

4. The country was an _____, because it was run by an all-powerful ruler.

5. Rome was a great _____ because it controlled many lands.

6. Christians, Muslims, and Jews follow _____, the belief in one god.

7. A _____ is a government with many different people making many decisions.

8. Many early people practiced _____, or the belief in many gods.

Vocabulary: World History, SV 9781419035029

Name _____ Date _____

Word Challenge: True or False

Write **T** next to each sentence that is true. Write **F** next to each sentence that is false. Rewrite each false sentence. The first one has been done for you.

1. __F__ An **ancient** piece of furniture could have been made in the past ten years.

   An ancient piece of furniture was made a thousand years ago.

2. _____ Early Greeks practiced **polytheism** because they believed in one god.

   _____

3. _____ A **dynasty** is a period of time when a country is ruled by leaders from the same family.

   _____

4. _____ You can use evidence to **verify** if something is true.

   _____

Word Challenge: What's Your Answer?

Read each question and write an answer on the line. Answer the questions in complete sentences. The first one has been done for you.

1. Where would a **pharaoh** have lived? _____ *A pharaoh would have lived in Egypt.*

2. What kind of information is **relevant** to your life? _____

   _____

3. Why might politicians and citizens want less **bureaucracy**? _____

   _____

4. What is the most important belief in **monotheism**? _____

   _____

Name _____ Date _____

Word Connections

Write at the top of the circle the words from the box that connect to the word or idea in the center. Write the words that do not connect in the area at the bottom.

relevant pharaoh	autocracy monotheism	bureaucracy verify

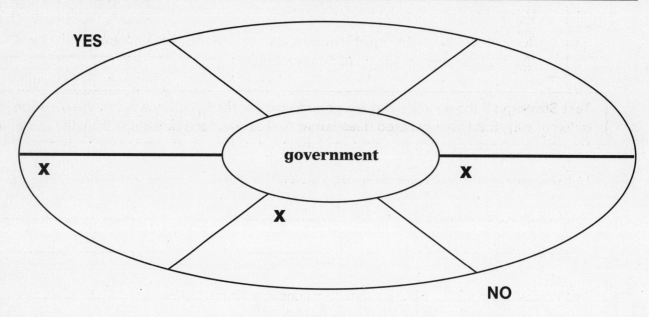

Word Study: The Prefixes *mono-* and *poly-*

When the prefixes *mono-* and *poly-* are added to a word, such as *tone*, they change the meaning of the word. *Mono-* means "one" or "single." *Poly-* means "many."

tone (n.) the pitch or sound of a voice
monotone (n.) made up of one tone
polytone (n.) made up of many tones

Circle each root word. Underline the prefixes *mono-* and *poly-*. Write a sentence for each word. Use a dictionary if you need help.

1. monosyllable _____

2. polysyllable _____

3. monotheism _____

4. polytheism _____

The Language of Testing

How would you answer a question like this on a test?

Which of the following describes the word *bureaucracy?*

(A) the rules of a government department
(B) a government ruled by one person
(C) leadership by the people
(D) a government made up of family members

Tip

The phrase *which of the following* means that you need to choose one of the answers listed (A, B, C, or D) to answer the question.

Test Strategy: If the question has the phrase *which of the following* in it, ask the question in a different way. Start your restated question with *what, who,* or *where.*

1. How could you say the question above in a different way?

_____

_____

Try the strategy again by asking these questions in a different way.

2. Which of the following is not a true statement about a pharaoh?

(A) Pharaohs were rulers.
(B) Pharaohs were Egyptian.
(C) Pharaohs ruled long ago.
(D) Pharaohs were always female.

3. Which of the following words is not related to leading a country?

(A) autocracy
(B) polytheism
(C) dynasty
(D) bureaucracy

Name _____ Date _____

On Your Own

Answer the questions.

1. What do you have that is **ancient**? _____

_____

2. Who is in charge in an **autocracy**? _____

_____

3. What is a **bureaucracy** made of? _____

_____

4. What would it be like to lead a **dynasty**? _____

_____

5. What are some **empires** you've learned about? _____

_____

6. What religions are based on **monotheism**? _____

_____

7. What might a **pharaoh's** life be like? _____

_____

8. What religions are based on **polytheism**? _____

_____

Write On!

You are a member of a ruling dynasty in an ancient civilization and have just taken power. On another sheet of paper, write a short plan for how you will rule. Include four specific policies about your type of government, religion, and/or general rules. Use four or more words from the lesson correctly in your plan.

ancient	autocracy	bureaucracy	dynasty	empire
monotheism	pharaoh	polytheism	relevant	verify

Name _____   Date _____

Lesson 2 Assessment

Read the sentences. Look for the best word to complete each sentence. Fill in the circle for the answer you choose. The first one has been done for you.

1. The ancient Egyptians practiced a _____ religion and believed in nearly 2,000 gods.
   - Ⓐ monotheistic
   - 🅑 polytheistic
   - Ⓒ autocratic
   - Ⓓ bureaucratic

2. The Middle East was the location of many _____ civilizations.
   - Ⓐ verified
   - Ⓑ pharaoh
   - Ⓒ empire
   - Ⓓ ancient

3. The Ming _____ ruled China for 275 years.
   - Ⓐ theocracy
   - Ⓑ polytheism
   - Ⓒ dynasty
   - Ⓓ pharaoh

4. The Jews of ancient Israel may have been the first people to practice _____.
   - Ⓐ polytheism
   - Ⓑ autocracy
   - Ⓒ bureaucracy
   - Ⓓ monotheism

5. Tutankhamen, also known as King Tut, is one of the most famous _____ of Egyptian history.
   - Ⓐ pharaohs
   - Ⓑ empires
   - Ⓒ relevancies
   - Ⓓ dynasties

6. Archaeologists _____ the history of ancient civilizations by studying artifacts.
   - Ⓐ domesticate
   - Ⓑ verify
   - Ⓒ migrate
   - Ⓓ bureaucrat

7. In _____, one person holds all the power.
   - Ⓐ a polytheism
   - Ⓑ a bureaucracy
   - Ⓒ an autocracy
   - Ⓓ a monotheism

8. Alexander the Great ruled a vast _____ that included ancient Greece, Egypt, and Persia.
   - Ⓐ monotheism
   - Ⓑ empire
   - Ⓒ polytheism
   - Ⓓ pharaoh

9. The writings of ancient civilizations are sometimes still _____ in today's society.
   - Ⓐ monotheistic
   - Ⓑ polytheistic
   - Ⓒ migrated
   - Ⓓ relevant

10. When you get a driver's license, you have to deal with government _____.
    - Ⓐ bureaucracy
    - Ⓑ autocracy
    - Ⓒ relevance
    - Ⓓ polytheism

Lesson 3

Name _____ Date _____

Greek and Roman Civilizations

Read the passage below. Think about the meaning of the words printed in **bold**. Underline any words that end with -cy. Remember that -cy names a type of government. Write what you think each word means near it. The first one has been done for you.

Ancient Greece

Vocabulary Strategy

Use familiar prefixes and suffixes to help you understand the meanings of new words.

government of wealthy people

Athens was the most important city of ancient Greece. At one time, Athens was an **aristocracy**, a government that is controlled by rich people, or aristocrats. Later, Athens became the world's first **democracy**, a government that is ruled by all people. Rich people and poor people had the same right to vote and make laws in Athens.

Like other people long ago, the Greeks believed in many gods. They told interesting stories called myths about their gods. These ancient stories have been **paraphrased**, or rewritten, in simple language.

Children today enjoy reading these very old stories.

The Greeks also studied **philosophy**. Philosophy is the study of ideas about knowledge and life. One part of Greek philosophy said it was important to develop both a strong mind and a strong body.

The Greeks also spoke about their ideas in public. Many Greeks used **rhetoric** to convince others that they had the right ideas about knowledge and life.

New World History Words

aristocracy
noun   a class of people who have a high position in society

democracy
noun   a system of government in which people choose their own laws and leaders

philosophy
noun   the study of ideas

rhetoric
noun   the use of language to convince people about something

Name _____ Date _____

Now read this passage and underline any words that begin with *pre-* or *de-*. Write what you think each of the underlined words means next to it. Remember that *pre-* means *before*, and *de-* means *down*.

Ancient Rome

The city of Rome began in Italy about 2,500 years ago. The Romans built the largest empire in the ancient world. They believed their empire would last forever. The Romans could not **predict** that after 800 years, their empire would break apart.

The Romans did not want to be ruled by a king or queen, so they started a government that was a **republic**. In a republic, people vote for their leaders. But rich Romans had more power in the government than poor people. Sometimes the leader of the government was a **dictator**. A dictator has full power to lead the army and make laws.

While the Roman Empire grew larger, the Christian religion began. The new religion was based on the teachings of Jesus. Jesus was a Jew who taught people to believe in one God. He also stressed the importance of **ethics**, or beliefs and rules about what is right and wrong.

The huge Roman Empire slowly **declined**, or grew weaker. About 1,500 years ago, the Roman empire broke apart.

More New World History Words

decline

verb   to become less in amount or importance

noun   a process by which something becomes less in amount or importance

dictator

noun   a leader who has total control of a country

ethics

noun   beliefs and rules about what is right and wrong

republic

noun   a country where people have the power

Our **republic** is shrinking.

I **predict** we are in a terrible **decline**.

Apply the Strategy

Look at a chapter in your textbook that your teacher identifies. Use familiar prefixes and suffixes to help you figure out the meaning of any new words you find.

Other Useful Words

paraphrase

verb   to reword something spoken or written

predict

verb   to say what will happen in the future

Name _____   Date _____

 Matching

Finish the sentences in Group A with words from Group B.

Group A

1. Julius Caesar is called a _____ because he had total control of Rome.

2. The Greeks invented _____ when they began to choose their leaders.

3. Politicians use _____ in their speeches to convince people to vote for them.

4. Can you _____ what the weather will be like tomorrow?

5. The Greek thinker Socrates shared his _____ about life in a dialogue with Plato.

Group B

A. democracy
B. dictator
C. predict
D. philosophy
E. rhetoric

Group A

6. People consider _____ when they make important decisions about life.

7. When people had a role in government, Rome was called a _____.

8. Roman society was broken up into classes with the _____ at the top and slaves at the bottom.

9. Possible reasons for the _____ of the Roman empire include money and military problems.

10. Persis _____ the long book for me so I would not have to read the whole thing.

Group B

F. aristocracy
G. decline
H. paraphrased
I. ethics
J. republic

Name _____   Date _____

Word Challenge: What's Your Answer?

Read each question and write an answer on the line. Answer the questions with complete sentences. The first one has been done for you.

1. When might you use **rhetoric**? <u>I use rhetoric when I want to convince</u>

   <u>someone.</u>

2. What rights might you lose if you lived in a country ruled by a **dictator**? _____

   _____

3. What is one characteristic of a **democracy**? _____

   _____

4. Who has the power in a **republic**? _____

   _____

Word Challenge: Which Word?

Think of a statement for each word below that gives a clue about its meaning. Write your statement next to the word. The first one has been done for you.

1. **aristocracy** <u>"I am a member of a wealthy and powerful class."</u>

2. **ethics** _____

3. **paraphrase** _____

4. **philosophy** _____

Name _____ Date _____

Synonyms and Antonyms

Write either a synonym or an antonym for the vocabulary words below. In some cases, you might be able to write both.

	Synonym	Antonym
1. aristocracy		
2. decline		
3. democracy		
4. dictator		

Word Study: The Suffixes -er and -or

When the suffix -er or -or is added to a root verb such as *dictate*, it does two things:

- First, it changes the part of speech from a verb to a noun: *dictator*.
- Second, it changes the meaning of the word. The new word names a person or thing that does a job.

dictate (v.) to order or command
dictator (n.) a person who rules a country with total control

Add -er or -or to the words below. Write the new word. Give the meaning of the new word you made. Use a dictionary to check your spelling and definitions.

	+ -er or -or	Definition
1. predict		
2. philosophy		
3. empire		
4. cultivate		

www.harcourtschoolsupply.com

© Harcourt Achieve Inc. All rights reserved.

26

Lesson 3: Greek and Roman Civilizations
Vocabulary: World History, SV 9781419035029

Name _____ Date _____

The Language of Testing

How would you answer a question like this on a test?

Each of the following statements is true

except

   (A) Rhetoric is used in persuasive speeches.

   (B) A dictator has total control.

   (C) A philosophy is a rule about what is right and wrong.

   (D) Aristocrats hold a high position in society.

Tip

The word *except* means you should look for something that means the opposite of the word or phrase before *except*. The opposite of true is false. So in this question, you should look for the answer that is false.

Test Strategy: Make sure you understand the question. Read it carefully. Then, if it has the word *except* in it, ask the question in a different way. Remember that you are looking for the statement that is false.

1. How could you say the question above in a different way?

_____

_____

Try the strategy again by asking these questions in a different way.

2. Each of these words is related to government except

   (A) dictator

   (B) democracy

   (C) republic

   (D) philosophy

3. All of these words describe aristocrats except

   (A) middle-class

   (B) noble

   (C) powerful

   (D) upper-class

Name _____ Date _____

 On Your Own

Answer the questions.

1. What does someone who is part of the **aristocracy** do? _____
   _____

2. Why does something **decline**? _____
   _____

3. What makes a **democracy** different from other kinds of government? _____
   _____

4. How does a **dictator** come to power? _____
   _____

5. What are your personal **ethics**? _____
   _____

6. What would you learn about if you studied **philosophy**? _____
   _____

7. What are some features of a **republic**? _____
   _____

8. When do you usually use **rhetoric**? _____
   _____

 Write On!

You are an ancient Greek philosopher who is speaking to the people of Athens about the importance of helping the poor people of the city. On another sheet of paper, write a brief speech in which you try to convince your fellow citizens that it is necessary to aid the poor. Be sure to write at least three convincing arguments and use at least four words from the lesson correctly.

aristocracy	**decline**	**democracy**	**dictator**	**ethics**
paraphrase	**philosophy**	**predict**	**republic**	**rhetoric**

Name _____   Date _____

Lesson 3 Assessment

Read the sentences. Look for the best word to complete each sentence. Fill in the circle for the answer you choose. The first one has been done for you.

1. Fighting among cities during the Peloponnesian War led to the _____ of ancient Greece.
   - Ⓐ philosophy
   - Ⓑ ethics
   - Ⓒ decline
   - Ⓓ republic

2. In the ancient Greek city of Sparta, only the _____, or wealthy landowners, had power.
   - Ⓐ aristocracy
   - Ⓑ dictators
   - Ⓒ republics
   - Ⓓ ethics

3. The Roman _____ was governed by senators who were elected by the people.
   - Ⓐ dictator
   - Ⓑ republic
   - Ⓒ aristocracy
   - Ⓓ philosophy

4. Julius Caesar was the first _____ of the Roman empire.
   - Ⓐ aristocracy
   - Ⓑ dictator
   - Ⓒ democracy
   - Ⓓ rhetoric

5. A fortuneteller _____ the death of Julius Caesar by telling him "Beware the Ides of March."
   - Ⓐ paraphrased
   - Ⓑ verified
   - Ⓒ cultivated
   - Ⓓ predicted

6. A sense of _____ is very important in most religions.
   - Ⓐ democracy
   - Ⓑ philosophy
   - Ⓒ ethics
   - Ⓓ rhetoric

7. When you _____ something, you tell only the important points.
   - Ⓐ predict
   - Ⓑ paraphrase
   - Ⓒ domesticate
   - Ⓓ verify

8. Ancient Athens was the world's first _____, giving all free male citizens the right to vote.
   - Ⓐ philosophy
   - Ⓑ dictator
   - Ⓒ autocracy
   - Ⓓ democracy

9. The beliefs of Socrates, Plato, and Aristotle are still taught in _____ classes.
   - Ⓐ philosophy
   - Ⓑ democracy
   - Ⓒ republic
   - Ⓓ aristocracy

10. Cicero is known as one of the greatest users of _____ because of his ability to persuade people.
    - Ⓐ monotheism
    - Ⓑ dictator
    - Ⓒ rhetoric
    - Ⓓ aristocracy

Name _____ Date _____

Medieval Life in Europe

Read the passage below. Think about the meanings of the new words printed in **bold**. Underline each definition and draw a line from it to the word it defines. The first one has been done for you.

Life in the Middle Ages

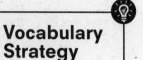
The years in Europe from 500 to 1500 were called the Middle Ages. They were also called **medieval** times. During this time, kings became less powerful.

A system called **feudalism** began during this period. Under this system, kings gave land to nobles. In return, nobles promised that their soldiers would fight for the king. The nobles also promised to protect the people who worked on their land. The large house and the land that belonged to the noble were called the **manor**. A manor had a church, farms, and a village.

During the Middle Ages, the Catholic Church became very powerful. Most people in Europe belonged to the church. But some people did not agree with Catholic teachings and tried to **refute** them. Catholic leaders called people who did not follow its teachings **heretics**. Many heretics were punished during the Middle Ages.

New World History Words

feudalism
noun   a system in which people were given land to work on and were protected by people with more power

heretic
noun   someone whose beliefs and actions go against accepted beliefs

manor
noun   a large country house on a large area of land with several smaller buildings around it

medieval
adjective   describing something belonging to the period of time in Europe between A.D. 476 and A.D. 1500

Name _____   Date _____

Now read the passage below and practice the strategy again. Underline *four* definitions in the text that can help you figure out what the words in bold print mean.

Life Under Feudalism

The feudal system had a **hierarchy**, or arrangement of people in order of power. At the top of the hierarchy was the king. Below the king was the **nobility**. The nobility were the nobles, or people who were of a high rank in society. Many nobles owned land. They also swore loyalty to the king. At the bottom of the hierarchy were **peasants**. These were poor people who farmed the land and lived on the manor in houses that had only one or two rooms. Peasants could not leave the manor unless the nobles allowed them to do so.

A system of **chivalry** developed in medieval times. Many rules were **formulated**, or developed, that explained how knights should behave. Knights were the soldiers who fought for the nobles. The rules of chivalry told the knight how to behave, how to be loyal, and how to be brave.

I've **formulated** a plan for us to go have some fun!

Sorry. I promised to mind my **manors**.

More New World History Words

chivalry

   noun   the rules that knights were required to follow

hierarchy

   noun   a way of organizing people into different levels of importance

nobility

   noun   a group of people in society who have a high rank

peasant

   noun   a person of lower rank that works on the land

Apply the Strategy

Look at a chapter in your textbook that your teacher identifies. Use definitions in the text to help you figure out the meaning of any new words you find.

Other Useful Words

formulate

   verb   to plan or develop something

refute

   verb   to prove that something or someone is wrong

Name _____ Date _____

The Right Word

Read each sentence. Look at the word or phrase that is underlined. Write a word from the box that means the same or almost the same as the underlined part of the sentence.

chivalry	**feudalism**	**heretics**	**hierarchy**
manors	**medieval**	**nobility**	**peasant**

1. _____ A system in which people lived and worked on manors was common during the Middle Ages.

2. _____ A low-ranking person who worked on the land would have worked for the nobility.

3. _____ The wealthy landowners lived in large houses with several smaller buildings around them.

4. _____ In the Middle Ages, people who disagreed with accepted beliefs were punished by the church.

5. _____ The high-ranking people were often wealthy landowners.

6. _____ Feudalism and knighthood were part of Middle Ages Europe.

7. _____ Knights were bound to a certain behavior by a code of rules.

8. _____ Social life in England in the Middle Ages followed a strict method of organizing people into different levels of importance.

Name _____ Date _____

Word Challenge: Which Word?

Think of a statement for each word below that gives a clue about its meaning. Write your statement next to the word. The first one has been done for you.

1. **nobility** _"We're second only to the king in society."_

2. **formulate** _____

3. **chivalry** _____

4. **heretic** _____

Word Challenge: What's Your Answer?

Read each question and write an answer on the line. Answer the questions with complete sentences. The first one has been done for you.

1. The man was accused of being a **heretic**. How do you think people felt

   about him? _They probably feared him._

2. What might the life of a **peasant** have been like during the Middle Ages?

   _____

3. Who might own a **manor**? _____

   _____

4. Why might someone **refute** a news report? _____

   _____

Name _____ Date _____

Extend the Meaning

Write the letter of the word or phrase that best completes the sentence.

1. **Feudalism** is a system related to _____.
   a. banking
   b. land
   c. wars

2. **Chivalry** is a set of rules for _____.
   a. landowners
   b. knights
   c. peasants

3. The **hierarchy** told who was most _____.
   a. knowledgeable
   b. important
   c. brave

4. **Medieval** is a term that relates to a period of time in _____.
   a. Asia
   b. America
   c. Europe

Word Study: The Suffixes -er and -est

When the suffixes *-er* and *-est* are added to a root adjective such as *noble,* they change the adjective's meaning and use.

- The suffix *-er* is used to compare two things: *noble, nobler.*
- The suffix *-est* is used to compare three or more things: *noble, nobler, noblest.*

noble (adj.) righteous
nobler (adj.) more righteous
noblest (adj.) most righteous

A. Add *-er* and *-est* to the words below. Use a dictionary to check your spelling.

Adjective	Comparative Adjective (+ -er)	Superlative Adjective (+ -est)
1. **fine**		
2. **rich**		
3. **sharp**		

B. Tell whether the sentence is comparing two things or three or more things.

1. The comb was the finest she'd ever seen. _____

2. The chocolate cake was richer than the banana cake. _____

3. She chose the sharpest of the four pencils to write her essay. _____

Name _____ Date _____

The Language of Testing

How would you answer a question like this on a test?

What is a **characteristic** of a heretic?

    (A) His or her beliefs are different from most.

    (B) He or she refuses to fight in a war.

    (C) He or she has a lot of money and power.

    (D) He or she is paid to give advice.

Tip

A *characteristic* of a thing is something it usually has or does.

Test Strategy: If you see a question that asks for a *characteristic* of something, rewrite it to ask for the thing that is true about something.

---

1. How could you say the question above in a different way?

_____

_____

Try the strategy again by asking these questions in a different way.

2. What is a characteristic of a peasant?

    (A) He or she works on the land.

    (B) He or she works in a store.

    (C) He or she works on a ship.

    (D) He or she works in a factory.

3. A characteristic of a feudal hierarchy is that

    (A) some people behave in ways that go against society.

    (B) knights have to follow a set of rules.

    (C) some people work on the land.

    (D) peasants give land to nobles.

Name _____ Date _____

On Your Own

Answer the questions.

1. What are some examples of **chivalry** today? _____
_____

2. What might it have been like to live under **feudalism**? _____
_____

3. Who might be considered a **heretic** today? _____
_____

4. What is the **hierarchy** in your school? _____
_____

5. What was life like on a **manor** for a worker? _____
_____

6. What would you miss if you lived in **medieval** times? _____
_____

7. What would you be like if you were part of the **nobility**? _____
_____

8. What might the life of a **peasant** be like? _____
_____

Write On!

You are a medieval knight in charge of formulating a code of chivalry for your fellow knights.
On another sheet of paper, write an essay in which you include at least four rules of chivalry.
Be sure to explain each rule thoroughly and use at least four words from the lesson correctly.

chivalry	feudalism	formulate	heretic	hierarchy
manor	medieval	nobility	peasant	refute

Name _____   Date _____

Lesson 4 Assessment

Read the sentences. Look for the best word to complete each sentence. Fill in the circle for the answer you choose. The first one has been done for you.

1. Knights, ladies-in-waiting, and castles are symbols of _____ times.
   Ⓐ heretic
   Ⓑ peasant
   Ⓒ nobility
   🅓 medieval

2. Polite, respectful behavior toward women was one of the rules of _____.
   Ⓐ feudalism
   Ⓑ chivalry
   Ⓒ hierarchy
   Ⓓ nobility

3. Many religious _____ were punished by the Catholic Church.
   Ⓐ peasants
   Ⓑ heretics
   Ⓒ manors
   Ⓓ nobility

4. The _____ of the Middle Ages was the king, the nobility, and the peasants.
   Ⓐ chivalry
   Ⓑ medieval
   Ⓒ manor
   Ⓓ hierarchy

5. The _____ and the peasants who worked on it were the property of the noble.
   Ⓐ manor
   Ⓑ nobility
   Ⓒ hierarchy
   Ⓓ chivalry

6. Jean _____ a plan to study for the exam.
   Ⓐ refuted
   Ⓑ predicted
   Ⓒ formulated
   Ⓓ differentiated

7. As a _____ in the Middle Ages, Steven could not own his own land.
   Ⓐ noble
   Ⓑ manor
   Ⓒ peasant
   Ⓓ knight

8. Because of _____, Lord Hastings was given a large amount of land in return for loyalty to the king.
   Ⓐ feudalism
   Ⓑ chivalry
   Ⓒ nobility
   Ⓓ peasants

9. The defendant _____ the accusation against him by providing a solid alibi.
   Ⓐ formulated
   Ⓑ refuted
   Ⓒ verified
   Ⓓ predicted

10. The _____ in the Middle Ages did not have to work to provide their own food.
    Ⓐ peasants
    Ⓑ manors
    Ⓒ nobility
    Ⓓ heretics

www.harcourtschoolsupply.com
© Harcourt Achieve Inc. All rights reserved.

37

Lesson 4: Medieval Life in Europe
Vocabulary: World History, SV 9781419035029

Name _____ Date _____

The Middle Ages

Read the passage below. Think about the meanings of the new words printed in **bold**. Circle any synonyms for the new words. Draw an arrow from each synonym to the new word it describes. The first one has been done for you.

The Crusades Change Europe

In 1095, Pope Urban II wanted to win control of the Holy Land from the ruling Turks. He especially wanted to gain control of Jerusalem. Jerusalem is now the capital of Israel. He called for a Crusade, or a war to win control of the Holy Land. Thousands of people joined the battle for the Holy Land. In 1097, the first army of Crusaders left Europe. Their goal was the **conquest** of all of the Holy Land. There were many Crusades during the next 200 years.

The Crusaders won control of the Holy Land for only a short time, but they brought changes to Europe. One change was that money became more important. Before the Crusades, the **barter** system was often used instead of money. When people bartered, they exchanged one kind of good for another. As the Crusades increased trade between Europe and Asia, however, money became a better way to pay for goods.

Learning also became more important. Europeans learned more about eastern cultures. Some **scholars** studied the works of ancient Greek philosophers. They **rephrased** these works into a variety of modern languages so other scholars could read them.

Vocabulary Strategy

Look for synonyms to help you figure out the meaning of new words. Look for clues like *or* to help you find synonyms in a text.

New World History Words

barter
  verb   to trade goods for other goods

conquest
  noun   the act of taking over a country
       or group of people

crusade
  noun   a long effort to achieve
       something for a cause
  verb   to fight hard to achieve
       something for a cause

scholar
  noun   a person who studies a subject
       and knows a great deal about it

Name _____ Date _____

Now read the passage below and practice the strategy again. Underline any synonyms that will help you figure out the meanings of the new words.

Other Changes During the Middle Ages

During the Middle Ages, **guilds** became important in Europe. A guild was an organization of workers who had the same kind of business or trade. Some of the guilds were for bakers and glassmakers. The guilds made rules about prices and salaries.

A person who wanted to learn a trade would start by becoming an **apprentice**. An apprentice learned a trade by living and working with a master of that trade for a number of years. For example, a baker's apprentice would learn to bake bread.

The Middle Ages also brought years of a terrible illness called the **plague** to Europe and to Asia. The disease spread quickly from one person to another. The plague killed more than 23 million people in Europe.

At the end of the Middle Ages, some people were not happy with the Catholic Church. They **reacted** by starting different churches. These churches became the first Protestant churches. Some of the Protestant leaders believed that the best government should be a **theocracy**. In a theocracy, religious leaders control the government and make the laws.

More New World History Words

apprentice

noun   a young person who works for no pay to learn a skill

guild

noun   an organization of people who do the same job or work at the same skill

plague

noun   a deadly disease that spreads very quickly

theocracy

noun   a society that is ruled by a religious figure

If you want to be my **apprentice**, you must speak the language of my **guild**.

Could you **rephrase** that?

Other Useful Words

react

verb   to respond in a certain way because of something that has happened to you

rephrase

verb   to say something in a different way

Apply the Strategy

Look at a chapter in your textbook that your teacher identifies. Find synonyms in the text to help you figure out the meaning of any new words you find.

Name _____ Date _____

Find the Word

Write a word from the box next to each clue. Then write the word formed by the boxed letters to finish the sentence below.

conquest	**apprentice**	**guild**	**barter**
theocracy	**crusade**	**scholar**	

1. a group of people who do the same work ___ ___ ___ ___ ☐

2. a young person who works to learn a skill ___ ___ ___ ___ ___ ☐ ___ ___ ___

3. the act of taking over a country ___ ___ ___ ___ ___ ☐ ___ ___

4. a long effort for a cause ___ ___ ___ ___ ___ ___ ☐

5. a society ruled by a religious figure ___ ___ ___ ___ ☐ ___ ___

6. a person who knows a lot about a subject ☐ ___ ___ ___ ___ ___ ___

7. to trade goods for other goods ___ ___ ___ ___ ☐ ___

The **plague** is a deadly ___ ___ ___ ___ ___ ___ ___.

Vocabulary: World History, SV 9781419035029

Name _____ Date _____

Word Challenge: Quick Pick

Read each question. Think of a response and write it on the line. Explain your answer.
The first one has been done for you.

1. Which is a **conquest**: winning a sports game or taking over a country? _Taking over a_
   country is a conquest.

2. Is a society ruled by a religious figure a **theocracy** or an autocracy?_____

   _____

3. Is a **guild** a group of people who are from the same family or who do the same job? _____

   _____

4. Which would be of more interest to a **scholar**: a library or a sports field? _____

   _____

Word Challenge: What's Your Answer?

Read each question and write an answer. Answer each question in a complete sentence.
The first one has been done for you.

1. Would you be an **apprentice** if you received a weekly salary for your work?
   I wouldn't be an apprentice because apprentices don't get paid.

2. Would you be **bartering** if you paid $25 for a sweater? _____

   _____

3. Would you be a **scholar** if you knew a lot about a subject? _____

   _____

4. If someone you knew had the **plague**, what would you do? _____

   _____

Analogies

Use a word from the box to finish each sentence. Write the word on the line.

apprentice	barter	plague	theocracy

1. Master is to _____ as teacher is to student.

2. Religious leader is to _____ as president is to democracy.

3. Deadly is to _____ as smelly is to garbage.

4. Trade is to _____ as revise is to change.

 Word Study: The *-ing* Ending

When the *-ing* ending is added to a noun such as *crusade*, it does two things:
- First, it makes the noun a verb: *crusading*.
- Second, it changes the word's meaning. The word now describes doing something.

Drop the *-e* from the end of a word before adding *-ing*.

crusade (n.) a long effort to achieve something for a cause
crusading (v.) making a long effort to achieve something for a cause

Add *-ing* to the words below. Give the meaning of the new word you made. Use a dictionary to check your spelling and definitions.

	+ *-ing*	Definition
1. **barter**		
2. **apprentice**		
3. **react**		
4. **rephrase**		

Name _____   Date _____

The Language of Testing

How would you answer a question like this on a test?

What is **the main purpose of** a *crusade*?

   Ⓐ to learn a new trade

   Ⓑ to meet new people

   Ⓒ to achieve something for a cause

   Ⓓ to visit a new place and learn about the people

Tip
The word *purpose* can mean *reason* or *use*. The word *main* means *most important*.

Test Strategy: If you see a question that uses the word *purpose*, rewrite it using the word *reason*, *function*, or *use*. If the question also includes the word *main*, look for the most important reason or use.

1. How could you say the question above in a different way?

_____

_____

Try the strategy again by asking these questions in a different way.

2. What is the main purpose of a conquest?

   Ⓐ to take over a group of people

   Ⓑ to achieve something important

   Ⓒ to learn about a group of people

   Ⓓ to stop migration

3. For what purpose might someone hire an apprentice?

   Ⓐ to get an expert employee

   Ⓑ to teach someone new a craft

   Ⓒ to learn something new

   Ⓓ to get an employee to train others

Name _____ Date _____

 On Your Own

Answer the questions.

1. Whom would you like to be an **apprentice** to? Why? _____

_____

2. What have you **bartered** with friends? _____

_____

3. What is a **conquest** you have made recently? _____

_____

4. What might you start a **crusade** about? _____

_____

5. If you could form a **guild**, what would it be? Why? _____

_____

6. How can people protect against a **plague**? _____

_____

7. What makes you a **scholar**? _____

_____

8. Who is in charge in a **theocracy**? _____

_____

 Write On!

You are a member of the medieval Catholic Church, and you're trying to convince your fellow citizens to join the Crusade to the Holy Land. On another sheet of paper, write a brief speech in which you give at least four convincing arguments for joining the Crusade. Use at least four words from the lesson correctly in your speech.

apprentice	barter	conquest	crusade	guild
plague	react	rephrase	scholar	theocracy

Name _____ Date _____

Lesson 5 Assessment

Read the sentences. Look for the best word to complete each sentence. Fill in the circle for the answer you choose. The first one has been done for you.

1. Gwen _____ to the loud noise of the sirens by covering her ears with her hands.
   - Ⓐ crusaded
   - Ⓑ reacted
   - Ⓒ rephrased
   - Ⓓ bartered

2. The _____ spread quickly in crowded cities and led to the death of many people.
   - Ⓐ apprentice
   - Ⓑ conquest
   - Ⓒ plague
   - Ⓓ theocracy

3. The goal of the Crusades was the _____ of the Holy Land.
   - Ⓐ conquest
   - Ⓑ apprentice
   - Ⓒ plague
   - Ⓓ guild

4. Iran, which is ruled by a religious leader, is a modern-day _____ .
   - Ⓐ guild
   - Ⓑ scholar
   - Ⓒ crusade
   - Ⓓ theocracy

5. The _____ learned how to make candles from his master.
   - Ⓐ apprentice
   - Ⓑ scholar
   - Ⓒ guild
   - Ⓓ barter

6. Daniel belongs to a(n) _____ of shoemakers.
   - Ⓐ theocracy
   - Ⓑ apprentice
   - Ⓒ guild
   - Ⓓ crusade

7. The women _____ with each other to trade their goods.
   - Ⓐ rephrased
   - Ⓑ bartered
   - Ⓒ crusaded
   - Ⓓ reacted

8. Could you please _____ the question? I don't understand it.
   - Ⓐ react
   - Ⓑ rephrase
   - Ⓒ verify
   - Ⓓ refute

9. John is a(n) _____ of astronomy. He knows everything about it.
   - Ⓐ apprentice
   - Ⓑ crusader
   - Ⓒ scholar
   - Ⓓ plague

10. Yvonne went on a _____ to end world hunger.
   - Ⓐ conquest
   - Ⓑ theocracy
   - Ⓒ guild
   - Ⓓ crusade

Name _____ Date _____

Trade and Exploration

Read the passage below. Think about the meaning of the words printed in **bold**. Circle any words that end with -al, -ize, or -tion. Write what you think the word means next to it. Remember that -al means "related to," -ize means "to make," and -tion names a process. The first one has been done for you.

 ## The Commercial Revolution

During the 1300s, there were many changes in the way business was done in Europe. The many (commercial) changes, or business changes, were called the Commercial Revolution.

related to trade

We can **generalize** about many things of this period. To generalize about the Commercial Revolution, we must say that trade grew both between the countries of Europe and with other parts of the world. New **commodities**, or products, like silks and spices were brought to Europe from Asia. New trade routes developed, banking became important, and **navigation**, or planning a course for travel, improved.

An instrument called the **compass** improved navigation. The compass was invented in China. It uses a magnet to point out the directions north, south, east, and west. By using a compass, sailors could sail far from land with less chance of getting lost at sea.

Vocabulary Strategy

Use familiar prefixes and suffixes to help you understand the meanings of new words.

 ## New World History Words

commercial
  adjective   done for a profit

commodity
  noun   something that is sold or traded

compass
  noun   a tool that is used for finding directions

navigation
  noun   the process of planning a course for travel

Name _____ Date _____

Now read the passage below and practice the vocabulary strategy again. Underline two words printed in **bold** that end in *-ism*. Remember that *-ism* names a belief. Write what you think each word means near it.

A Changing World

The growth of trade between Europe and other parts of the world brought new ideas to Europe. The years from 1400 to 1700 were called the **Renaissance**, which means rebirth. This was a period of new ideas and learning.

England, Spain, and France followed a theory called **mercantilism**. According to this theory, a nation needs large amounts of gold and silver to be wealthy and strong. Nations would become wealthy by selling more goods to other countries than they

bought. Nations put **tariffs**, or taxes, on goods from other countries to prevent people from buying them.

During the 1500s, Europeans began trading in Japan. The leaders of Japan, however, started a policy of **isolationism** to keep Japan apart from other countries. We can **infer** that the Japanese leaders wanted to keep their own laws and customs. Isolationism lasted more than 200 years in Japan.

More New World History Words

isolationism

noun   a policy of avoiding contact with other countries

mercantilism

noun   a policy of building wealth through trade

renaissance

noun   a period of time during which there is a growth in learning and the arts, or the period in Europe from 1400 to 1700

tariff

noun   a tax that the government collects on imported goods

My **navigation** skills are terrible! We will be lost.

We can't get lost with this **compass**!

Apply the Strategy

Look at a chapter in your textbook that your teacher identifies. Use prefixes and suffixes to help you figure out the meaning of new words.

Other Useful Words

generalize

verb   to say something that is almost always true, or to leave out the details

infer

verb   to come to a conclusion

Name _____ Date _____

Categories

Write the words from the word bank in the correct boxes below. Some words may be used in more than one box.

| commercialism | commodity | compass | tariff |
| isolationism | mercantilism | navigation | |

Trade	Travel

Lesson 6: Trade and Exploration
Vocabulary: World History, SV 9781419035029

Name _____   Date _____

Word Challenge: Quick Pick

Read each question. Think of a response and write it on the line. Explain your answer.
The first one has been done for you.

1. Would a country with a policy of mercantilism trade with other countries or do battle with

    them? _It would trade with other countries._____

2. Is a country with closed borders **commercial**, or is it practicing **isolationism**?

    _____

3. Does **navigation** involve travel or shopping? _____

    _____

4. What would show a **renaissance** has happened: more art or more people? _____

    _____

Word Challenge: Correct or Incorrect

Write **C** if the sentence is correct, and write **I** if the sentence is incorrect. Rewrite the incorrect
sentences. The first one has been done for you.

1. __C__ The government collected a **tariff** on lamb from New Zealand.

2. _____ The cyclists used a **compass** to determine how far they had traveled.

    _____

3. _____ For our new business, we decided cellphones were a **commodity** that
    would sell well.

    _____

4. _____ Lee **inferred** from the empty plate and the paw prints that his dog had
    eaten his sandwich.

    _____

Synonyms

In each of the groups, circle the synonyms.

1.   commodity   tariff

      sale   product

2.   tariff   exchange

      tax   good

3.   exchange   trade

      purchase   commodity

4.   navigation   course-plotting

      compass   profit-making

Word Study: The Suffix -ion

When the suffix -ion is added to a verb such as navigate, it does two things:
- First, it changes the verb to a noun: navigation.
- Second, it changes the word's meaning. The new word names a process or result.

Drop the -e from the end of a word before adding -ion.

navigate (v.) to steer or plot a course
navigation (n.) the process of planning a course of travel

Add the suffix -ion to each root verb to make a new word. Then, write the definition of the new word. Use a dictionary to check your spelling and definitions.

	+ -ion	Definition
1. **isolate**		
2. **imitate**		
3. **reject**		

www.harcourtschoolsupply.com

50

Lesson 6: Trade and Exploration
Vocabulary: World History, SV 9781419035029

Name _____   Date _____

The Language of Testing

How would you answer a question like this on a test?

For many years, the Chinese government practiced isolationism. What does this **suggest** about the Chinese government?

Ⓐ It did not want relations with other countries.
Ⓑ It wanted to become rich from trade.
Ⓒ It was interested in exploration.
Ⓓ It valued profit over all else.

Tip

When the word *suggest* is used in a question, you should draw a conclusion about information in the question.

Test Strategy: If you see a question that uses the word *suggest*, rewrite it so that it asks you what the information probably means or what your conclusion is.

1. How could you say the question above in a different way?

_____

_____

Try the strategy again by asking these questions in a different way.

2. What does it suggest about a group of travelers if they pull out a compass?

Ⓐ They need to know the time.
Ⓑ They need directions.
Ⓒ They need to know how much farther they have to go.
Ⓓ They want to know how fast they're traveling.

_____

_____

_____

_____

3. What does it suggest if a business is required to pay a tariff?

Ⓐ It has sold goods to another country.
Ⓑ It has made a large profit.
Ⓒ It has exchanged goods with another business.
Ⓓ It has purchased goods from another country.

_____

_____

_____

_____

Name _____ Date _____

On Your Own

Answer the questions.

1. What are some bad things about **commercialism**? _____
   _____

2. What **commodity** would you like to sell? Why? _____
   _____

3. Describe a time when you wished you had a **compass**. _____
   _____

4. Why might a country have a policy of **isolationism**? _____
   _____

5. What are some features of **mercantilism**? _____
   _____

6. How do you use your **navigation** skills every day? _____
   _____

7. How would you know if your town was undergoing a **renaissance**? _____
   _____

8. When might a **tariff** be unfair? _____
   _____

Write On!

It is the year 1650, and you are a Japanese citizen who wants the country to end its policy of isolationism. On another sheet of paper, write a brief essay in which you try to convince the emperor to open the country up for trade and exploration. Be sure to write at least three convincing arguments and use at least four words from the lesson correctly.

commercial	commodity	compass	generalize	infer
isolationism	mercantilism	navigation	renaissance	tariff

Vocabulary: World History, SV 9781419035029

Lesson 6 Assessment

Read the sentences. Look for the best word to complete each sentence. Fill in the circle for the answer you choose. The first one has been done for you.

1. Improvements in _____ led to regular overseas trade between Europe and China.
   - Ⓐ commodities
   - Ⓑ mercantilism
   - Ⓒ navigation
   - Ⓓ isolationism

2. Salt was hard to obtain and was therefore a valuable _____ during the Middle Ages.
   - Ⓐ tariff
   - Ⓑ commodity
   - Ⓒ compass
   - Ⓓ renaissance

3. Many people _____ about the laziness of teenagers.
   - Ⓐ infer
   - Ⓑ differentiate
   - Ⓒ predict
   - Ⓓ generalize

4. The U.S. government placed a high _____ on foreign cars.
   - Ⓐ compass
   - Ⓑ navigation
   - Ⓒ renaissance
   - Ⓓ tariff

5. The _____ fishing industry is an important source of income for people who live along the Atlantic Ocean.
   - Ⓐ commercial
   - Ⓑ navigation
   - Ⓒ commodity
   - Ⓓ mercantilism

6. A country that practices _____ won't trade with any other countries.
   - Ⓐ mercantilism
   - Ⓑ navigation
   - Ⓒ isolationism
   - Ⓓ renaissance

7. A _____ is a period of new ideas and learning.
   - Ⓐ commodity
   - Ⓑ tariff
   - Ⓒ compass
   - Ⓓ renaissance

8. The mother saw her crying child and _____ that he was unhappy.
   - Ⓐ generalized
   - Ⓑ inferred
   - Ⓒ predicted
   - Ⓓ refuted

9. Countries that believe in _____ trade with other countries.
   - Ⓐ isolationism
   - Ⓑ mercantilism
   - Ⓒ renaissance
   - Ⓓ navigation

10. Rachel looked at her _____ and saw that she was traveling north.
   - Ⓐ navigation
   - Ⓑ tariff
   - Ⓒ compass
   - Ⓓ commodity

Lesson 7

Name _____ Date _____

Absolutism

Read the passage below. Think about the meanings of the new words printed in **bold**. Underline any familiar root words within some of the new words that might help you figure out what these words mean. Write what the root means near the word. The first one has been done for you.

monarch=king

Absolute Monarchies

Vocabulary Strategy

Use words you know to help unlock the meaning of unfamiliar words in the same family. For example, *settle* can help you unlock the meaning of *settlement*, *settler*, and *unsettled*. You can keep track of these word groups by making a Word Web.

In the 1400s, some nations in Europe were **monarchies**. A monarchy is a government that is ruled by a king or queen. Sometimes a king or queen is called a **sovereign**.

France, Spain, and Russia were three nations that had monarchs who believed in **absolutism**. Under absolutism, the king had absolute, or total, power to make all laws and decisions for the country. The king could decide by himself to raise taxes or to go to war against another country. Many absolute monarchs believed that God gave them the power to make all laws.

Total control of a country by a leader is also called **despotism**. It is a **fallacy**, or false idea, to think that all despots were bad leaders, however. Some of these leaders in the late 1700s made good laws to improve their countries. However, many despots were very cruel.

King Louis XIV of France

✔ New World History Words

absolutism
noun a system in which one ruler has total power over a country

despotism
noun cruel and unfair government by very powerful rulers

monarchy
noun a country that is ruled by a king or queen

sovereign
adjective to have the most power, or to be independent, especially in the case of a country
noun a royal ruler of a country

Now read this passage and practice the vocabulary strategy again. Circle familiar root words that are found in larger, unfamiliar words. Write the meaning of each circled root word near it.

A Different Kind of Monarchy

England also had a monarchy, but it was not an absolute monarchy. Starting in 1295, England had a group of lawmakers called **Parliament**. As time passed, Parliament had more and more power and the kings had less power. Today, a queen still **reigns**, or rules, in England, but all laws are made by Parliament.

From 1642 to 1660, there was no monarchy in England. Instead, a dictator named Oliver Cromwell ruled. After his death, a king began to rule England again. This period of time was called the **Restoration**.

Diplomacy also began in Europe in the 1400s. Diplomacy means representatives of nations work together to solve problems and create treaties. The job of the representatives is to **articulate**, or explain clearly, what their nation wants.

More New World History Words

diplomacy

noun   the process of developing good relationships between countries

parliament

noun   a group of people in some countries who make the laws

reign

verb   to rule or have power, especially over a country

noun   the period of time during which someone or a group rules

restoration

noun   the process of bringing something back or making something like new

Apply the Strategy

Look at a chapter in your textbook that your teacher identifies. Use familiar root words to help you figure out the meaning of any new words you find.

Other Useful Words

articulate

verb   to express thoughts clearly and easily

fallacy

noun   a false or mistaken idea

Name _____   Date _____

 The Right Word

Read each sentence. Look at the word or phrase that is underlined. Write a word from the box that means the same or almost the same as the underlined part of the sentence.

monarchy sovereign	despotism absolutism	diplomacy restoration	reign parliament

1. _____ The queen is expected to <u>rule over the country</u> for many years to come.

2. _____ In New Zealand, the <u>group of people who make the laws</u> works in a building shaped like a beehive.

3. _____ After many years in a dusty basement, the painting required <u>the process of making something like new</u>.

4. _____ Ambassadors from many countries in the world are chosen to perform <u>the job of maintaining good relations between countries</u>.

5. _____ Denmark has been a <u>country ruled by a king or queen</u> for more than one thousand years.

6. _____ The fascist leaders of World War II were known for their <u>cruel leadership</u>.

7. _____ The ideals of democracy do not allow for <u>a system in which one leader rules a country with total power</u>.

8. _____ After many years of British rule, India became <u>independent</u> in 1947.

Name _____   Date _____

Word Challenge: Which Word?

Think of a statement for each word below that gives a clue about its meaning. Write your statement next to the word. The first one has been done for you.

1. **absolutism** *"I'm a government with one ruler!"*

2. **articulate** _____

3. **fallacy** _____

4. **reign** _____

Word Challenge: Finish the Idea

Read the incomplete sentences below. Write an ending for each. The first one has been done for you.

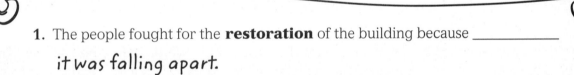

1. The people fought for the **restoration** of the building because _____
   it was falling apart.
   _____

2. **Diplomacy** is important because _____
   _____

3. Countries should fight **despotism** because _____
   _____

4. England is a **monarchy** because _____
   _____

Name _____ Date _____

Extend the Meaning

Write the letter of the word or phrase that best completes the sentence.

1. A _____ might **reign** over a country.
   a. shopkeeper
   b. leader
   c. public servant

2. A **restoration** might involve _____.
   a. tearing down an old house
   b. fixing up an old house
   c. buying a new house

3. A **sovereign** might _____.
   a. rule from a royal court
   b. be an assistant to a royal
   c. make clothes for royalty

4. **Diplomacy** might include _____.
   a. going to war
   b. finding the middle ground
   c. terrorizing innocent people

Word Study: The Suffix *-ism*

When the suffix *-ism* is added to a noun, such as *despot,* it changes the noun's meaning. The suffix *-ism* can express a belief, process, or practice. The word now refers to a belief or practice: *despotism.*

despot (n.) a powerful ruler who rules cruelly and unfairly
despotism (n.) cruel and unfair government by powerful rulers

Add *-ism* to the words below. If necessary, drop the *-e* from words before adding *-ism*. Then, write a definition of the new word. Use a dictionary to check your spelling and definitions.

	+ *-ism*	Definition
1. **absolute**		
2. **feudal**		
3. **isolation**		
4. **mercantile**		

Name _____ Date _____

The Language of Testing

How would you answer a question like this on a test?

Which of the following **compares closely to**
despotism?

    (A) autocracy

    (B) democracy

    (C) communism

    (D) socialism

Tip

The phrase *compares closely to* means *is most like.*

Test Strategy: If you see the phrase *compares closely to* on a test, rewrite it using the phrase *is most like.*

1. How could you say the question above in a different way?

    _____

    _____

Try the strategy again by asking these questions in a different way.

2. All of the following compare closely to the meaning of *restoration* except

    (A) restore

    (B) abolition

    (C) reinstate

    (D) return

3. What word compares closely to the meaning of *diplomacy*?

    (A) invasion

    (B) negotiation

    (C) cooperation

    (D) compromise

Vocabulary: World History, SV 9781419035029

Name _____   Date _____

On Your Own

Answer the questions.

1. What is the government like under **absolutism**? _____

_____

2. What would it be like to live under **despotism**? _____

_____

3. How do you practice **diplomacy** in your life? _____

_____

4. What would be some of the problems with living in a **monarchy**? _____

_____

5. What are some things that a **parliament** might do? _____

_____

6. How would you **reign** if you were in charge? _____

_____

7. What happens during a **restoration**? _____

_____

8. Why would a country want to be **sovereign**? _____

_____

Write On!

You are a citizen of a country that is ruled by a despot. You are at a secret meeting of citizens who want to get rid of the despot and establish another form of government. On another sheet of paper, write a short plan outlining the type of government you think would be best for your country. Be sure to use at least four words from the lesson correctly.

absolutism	**articulate**	**despotism**	**diplomacy**	**fallacy**
monarchy	**parliament**	**reign**	**restoration**	**sovereign**

Name _____ Date _____

Lesson 7 Assessment

Read the sentences. Look for the best word to complete each sentence. Fill in the circle for the answer you choose. The first one has been done for you.

1. Even though he practiced _____, Louis XIV made many laws that benefited the people of France.
   - Ⓐ diplomacy
   - 🅑 despotism
   - Ⓒ restoration
   - Ⓓ fallacy

2. The _____ of the old house cost a lot of money and took the workers nearly a year.
   - Ⓐ reign
   - Ⓑ sovereign
   - Ⓒ parliament
   - Ⓓ restoration

3. Many rulers who practiced _____ believed that their total control and power came directly from God.
   - Ⓐ diplomacy
   - Ⓑ absolutism
   - Ⓒ parliament
   - Ⓓ fallacy

4. Unable to _____ his thoughts, George kept silent.
   - Ⓐ articulate
   - Ⓑ reign
   - Ⓒ verify
   - Ⓓ infer

5. Saudi Arabia is ruled by a king; therefore, it is a _____ .
   - Ⓐ diplomacy
   - Ⓑ parliament
   - Ⓒ monarchy
   - Ⓓ fallacy

6. Elizabeth I of England _____ for 45 years.
   - Ⓐ articulated
   - Ⓑ reigned
   - Ⓒ formulated
   - Ⓓ generalized

7. The United Nations works to solve world problems through _____ instead of through military action.
   - Ⓐ despotism
   - Ⓑ diplomacy
   - Ⓒ absolutism
   - Ⓓ restoration

8. The British _____ serves the same function as the United States Congress.
   - Ⓐ Reign
   - Ⓑ Sovereign
   - Ⓒ Parliament
   - Ⓓ Monarch

9. In the Middle Ages, most people believed the _____ that the earth is flat.
   - Ⓐ generalization
   - Ⓑ diplomacy
   - Ⓒ reign
   - Ⓓ fallacy

10. A _____ nation is not a colony in another nation's empire.
    - Ⓐ sovereign
    - Ⓑ dictator
    - Ⓒ peasant
    - Ⓓ dynasty

Vocabulary: World History, SV 9781419035029

Name _____ Date _____

Expansion and Imperialism

Read the passage below. Think about the meaning of the words in **bold**.
Underline any familiar root words within some of the new words to help you
figure out what these words mean. Write the meaning of the root word near
the word in the passage. The first one has been done for you.

to grow

Empires and Colonies

Vocabulary Strategy

Use words you know to help unlock the meaning of unfamiliar words in the same family. For example, *expand* can help you unlock the meaning of *expansion*.

About the year 1300, Muslims won control of many parts of Asia, Africa, and the Middle East. Muslims follow the religion of Islam. The **expansion**, or growth, of Muslim empires brought Islam to many parts of the world.

At the end of the 1400s, explorers discovered new trade routes to Asia. In the 1600s, England gained control of **territory**, or land, in India.

Christopher Columbus was an explorer who sailed for Spain. His **strategy**, or plan, was to reach Asia by sailing west across the Atlantic Ocean. Instead of reaching Asia, however, Columbus reached the

Americas in 1492. The Americas were a new world to Europeans.

For many years, Spain, Britain, and France ruled **colonies** in the Americas. A colony is a country that is controlled by another nation. The Spanish wanted to teach the Catholic religion to the Native Americans in their colonies. The Spanish built many missions and sent **missionaries** to teach religion to the Native Americans.

New World History Words

colony

noun a settlement or land that belongs to another country

expansion

noun the act of becoming greater in size or amount

missionary

noun a person sent to a foreign place to teach about his or her religion

territory

noun land controlled by a country or ruler

Name _____ Date _____

Now read the passage below and practice the vocabulary strategy again. Underline any familiar words that are found in larger unfamiliar words. Write what these words mean near them in the passage.

Building Empires

During the 1600s and 1700s, England, Spain, and France won control of colonies in America. There was **rivalry**, or competition, between England and France to control the most colonies in America.

Many years later, between 1850 and 1914, **imperialism** became important in Europe. Imperialism means a nation takes control of colonies to build an empire. England ruled many colonies and had the world's largest empire.

Assimilation often took place in a colony. Some people in the colony took on the culture of the ruling nation. However, as colonists built their lives in other lands, their loyalties shifted to their new homes. They didn't want to be ruled by the old country anymore, but wanted to make the colonies into a new country. **Nationalism**, or a strong love and loyalty that people have for their own country, made them want to separate from the old country. Back home, however, the **perspective** was different. Owning colonies made the people in the old country feel powerful.

More New World History Words

assimilation

  noun   the act of learning or adopting the ideas, customs, and lifestyles of another culture

imperialism

  noun   a system in which a rich and powerful country has control over other countries

nationalism

  noun   strong feelings of loyalty to one's country

rivalry

  noun   competition or fighting

This **rivalry** for colonies is really getting out of hand!

Apply the Strategy

Look at a chapter in your textbook that your teacher identifies. Use familiar root words to help you figure out the meaning of new words you find.

Other Useful Words

perspective

  noun   a specific way of thinking about something

strategy

  noun   a plan for reaching a goal

Name _____ Date _____

Find the Word

Write a word from the box next to each clue. Then write the word formed by the boxed letters to complete the sentence below.

territory	assimilation	imperialism	colony
missionary	expansion	nationalism	

1. when one country controls others __ __ __ [ ] __ __ __ __ __

2. a country or region controlled by another __ __ __ __ [ ] __

3. getting bigger [ ] __ __ __ __ __ __ __ __

4. a religious teacher [ ] __ __ __ __ __ __ __ __

5. loyalty to one's country __ __ __ [ ] __ __ __ __ __ __

6. land controlled by a country or ruler __ [ ] __ __ __ __ __ __ __

7. adopting new customs __ [ ] __ __ __ __ __ __ __ __ __ __

People involved in a **rivalry** are often called __ __ __ __ __ __ __ .

Name _____   Date _____

Word Challenge: What's Your Answer?

Read each question and write an answer on the line. Answer the questions in complete sentences. The first one has been done for you.

1. What reason could you give for being against **imperialism**? _A stronger country_ _can take advantage of a weaker country under imperialism._

2. How would you feel if your country was a **colony** of another country? _____
   _____

3. How might you change if you faced **assimilation** in another country? _____
   _____

4. What **rivalry** are you involved with at school? _____
   _____

Word Challenge: Finish the Idea

Read the incomplete sentences below. Write an ending for each. The first one has been done for you.

1. A student needs a **strategy** for studying for a test because _he or she_
   might not study what is important.

2. I have a different **perspective** from my friend about the best sneakers because
   _____

3. **Missionaries** went to the new world because _____
   _____

4. **Nationalism** can lead to war because _____
   _____

Name _____ Date _____

Synonyms and Antonyms

Write either a synonym or an antonym for the vocabulary words below. In some cases, you might be able to provide both.

	Synonym	Antonym
1. assimilation		
2. colony		
3. expansion		
4. nationalism		
5. rivalry		

Word Study: The Suffix -ion

When the suffix -ion is added to a verb such as assimilate, it does two things:
- First, it makes a noun: assimilation.
- Second, the word now names a process.

Drop the -e from the end of the word before adding -ion.

assimilate (v.) to learn or adopt new customs
assimilation (n.) the act of learning or adopting new customs

Add the suffix -ion to each root verb to make a new word. Write a definition for each. Use a dictionary to check your spelling and your definitions.

	+ -ion	Definition
1. vibrate		
2. migrate		
3. vacate		
4. imitate		

Name _____   Date _____

The Language of Testing

How would you answer a question like this on a test?

What is a **characteristic** of a colony?

Ⓐ It rules other countries.

Ⓑ It is under the control of another country.

Ⓒ It has complete political independence.

Ⓓ It is always ruled by a king or queen.

Tip

A *characteristic* of a thing is something that it usually has or does.

Test Strategy: If you see a question that uses the word *characteristic*, rewrite it to ask for the thing that is true about the subject of the question.

---

1. How could you say the question above in a different way?

   _____

   _____

Try the strategy again by asking these questions in a different way.

2. What is a characteristic of missionaries?

   Ⓐ They are powerful rulers.

   Ⓑ They are religious teachers.

   Ⓒ They are fierce competitors.

   Ⓓ They are proud citizens.

   _____

   _____

   _____

   _____

   _____

3. What is a characteristic of nationalism?

   Ⓐ pride in one's country

   Ⓑ a desire to rule other countries

   Ⓒ learning new customs

   Ⓓ growing larger in size or amount

   _____

   _____

   _____

   _____

   _____

Name _____ Date _____

On Your Own

Answer the questions.

1. What happens during **assimilation**? _____
   _____

2. Name a country that built a **colony** in North America. _____
   _____

3. What problems can the **expansion** of a city cause? _____
   _____

4. How does **imperialism** change a country? _____
   _____

5. What kind of work does a **missionary** do? _____
   _____

6. How do people show their **nationalism**? _____
   _____

7. Whom do you have a **rivalry** with? _____
   _____

8. What places do you consider your **territory**? _____
   _____

Write On!

You are an explorer who has landed in the New World. On another sheet of paper, write a letter back to the ruling monarch of your home country outlining your logical strategy for creating a new settlement there. Be sure to include at least four details in your strategy and use four or more words from the lesson correctly.

assimilation	**colony**	**expansion**	**imperialism**	**missionary**
perspective	**nationalism**	**rivalry**	**strategy**	**territory**

Vocabulary: World History, SV 9781419035029

Name _____ Date _____

Lesson 8 Assessment

Read the sentences. Look for the best word to complete each sentence. Fill in the circle for the answer you choose.

1. The _____ of Muslim empires helped to spread the religion of Islam around the world.
   - (A) colony
   - (B) imperialism
   - (C) assimilation
   - (D) expansion

2. People have very different _____ on how the government should be run.
   - (A) perspectives
   - (B) territories
   - (C) rivalries
   - (D) assimilations

3. The _____ between the two boxers will be settled in the ring tonight.
   - (A) colony
   - (B) rivalry
   - (C) territory
   - (D) strategy

4. Many people undergo the process of _____ when they come to the United States.
   - (A) expansion
   - (B) nationalism
   - (C) assimilation
   - (D) imperialism

5. At one time, Australia was a _____ of the British empire.
   - (A) strategy
   - (B) colony
   - (C) missionary
   - (D) rivalry

6. _____ is very evident during both the summer and winter Olympic Games.
   - (A) Nationalism
   - (B) Isolationism
   - (C) Imperialism
   - (D) Expansion

7. Many _____ tried to spread Christianity in Africa.
   - (A) strategists
   - (B) imperialists
   - (C) nationalists
   - (D) missionaries

8. England's huge empire was a result of _____.
   - (A) nationalism
   - (B) assimilation
   - (C) imperialism
   - (D) missionaries

9. Alaska was a _____ of the United States before it became a state in 1959.
   - (A) strategy
   - (B) rivalry
   - (C) territory
   - (D) perspective

10. Christopher Columbus's _____ was to reach the East Indies by sailing west around the world.
    - (A) expansion
    - (B) strategy
    - (C) rivalry
    - (D) assimilation

Name _____ Date _____

Revolution and Change

Read the passage below. Think about the meaning of the new words printed in **bold**. Underline any words or phrases that contrast a word you know with a new word or idea. The first one has been done for you.

The French Revolution

A period called the **Enlightenment** took place during the 1600s and 1700s. The leaders of this period turned to science and reason rather than tradition and religion to solve problems. Unlike leaders of the past, they believed all people had the natural right to freedom. These ideas helped the United States win a war for freedom from Great Britain.

The French wanted more freedom, too. In 1789, the French Revolution began. France's king, Louis XVI, asked other countries to fight against the leaders of the French Revolution. The king had worked against the government, so he was found guilty of **treason** and killed.

In 1789, some French leaders were **moderates**. Unlike the **radicals**, they wanted to make some changes, but not too many, to improve the government. However, the radical leaders won control of the government.

These radicals completely changed the laws and government. The radicals said they believed in the ideas of the French Revolution. Two of those ideas were liberty and equality. The actions of the radicals **contradicted** these ideas, however. They had thousands of people killed for disagreeing with their ideas.

Vocabulary Strategy

Use contrasts to help you understand the meanings of new words. Look for clues that point out contrasts, such as *unlike*, *instead*, or *different from*.

New World History Words

enlightenment

noun   the act of giving or gaining knowledge about something, or the movement in the 18th century based on science and reason

moderate

adjective   avoiding extreme behavior or beliefs

noun   someone who avoids extreme behavior or beliefs

radical

adjective   showing extreme beliefs

noun   someone who has extreme beliefs

treason

noun   an action carried out to harm

Library of Congres

Name _____ Date _____

Now read the passage below and practice the strategy again. Underline any words or phrases that contrast something you know with a new word or idea. Look for clues that point out contrasts, like *unlike*, *instead*, or *different from*.

After the French Revolution

In 1789, Napoleon Bonaparte, a French army leader, became the ruler of France. Napoleon's army conquered many countries in Europe, and he chose new leaders for these countries. He was defeated in 1815.

In 1814, the leaders of France, England, Austria, and two other nations met in Vienna, Austria. Their meetings were called the Congress of Vienna. The meetings were **counterrevolutionary**. Their goal was to end all governments that had been started by the French Revolution and Napoleon.

The leader of the Congress of Vienna was Prince Metternich. He was **characterized**

as a person who wanted a lot of power. Unlike a radical, who wants change, he was a **conservative.** He did not agree with French Revolution ideas about freedom and equality.

The leaders in Vienna shared Metternich's ideas. They were **reactionaries**. Unlike revolutionaries, they wanted to make Europe the way it had been before 1789. In addition, they wanted to stop future revolutions. These leaders were also **royalists**. They did not want a democratic government, but instead planned to have their old kings and queens rule Europe again.

More New World History Words

conservative
noun   someone who resists change
adjective   resisting change

counterrevolutionary
adjective   about policies or people who want to reverse the effects of social or political change

reactionary
adjective   wanting to return to an older system
noun   a person who wants to return to an older system

royalist
noun   someone who supports rule by a king or queen

Congress of Vienna

Turning all clocks back won't **counter** the changes made by the **revolution**!

Apply the Strategy

Look at a chapter in your textbook that your teacher identifies. Use contrasts in the text to help you figure out the meaning of any new words you find.

Other Useful Words

characterize
verb   to describe someone or something by a specific thing

contradict
verb   to go against or say the opposite of something

Name _____   Date _____

 Categories

Sort the words printed in **bold** into the correct boxes below. Some words can be sorted into more than one box. The first word has been sorted for you.

conservative	**counterrevolutionary**	**characterize**	**contradict**	**radical**
moderate	**enlightenment**	**reactionary**	**royalist**	**treason**

Descriptions of Political Beliefs (adjectives)	Political and Cultural Beliefs (nouns)	Actions (verbs)
conservative	conservative	

Word Challenge: Would You/If You . . .

Read the following questions. Write an answer for each on the lines. The first one has been done for you.

1. Would you want to change the rules if you were **conservative**? _No. If I was_

conservative, I wouldn't want to change the rules.

2. Would you be committing **treason** if you joined the army? _____

_____

3. Would you become the best friend of a **radical** if you were a **reactionary**? _____

_____

4. Would you want to help a **counterrevolutionary** if you were a **moderate**? _____

_____

Word Challenge: Which Word?

Think of a statement for each word below that gives a clue about its meaning. Write your statement next to the word. The first one has been done for you.

1. **enlightenment** _"I used science and reason to solve problems!"_

2. **contradict** _____

3. **moderate** _____

4. **treason** _____

5. **reactionary** _____

Name _____   Date _____

Extend the Meaning

Write the letter of the word or phrase that best completes each sentence.

1. A **royalist** wants a government with a _____.

   a. nomad

   b. scholar

   c. monarch

2. If you lived during the **Enlightenment**, you would try to solve problems using _____.

   a. science

   b. religion

   c. tradition

3. When you **contradict** your friend, you _____.

   a. make a statement that is the opposite of what your friend says

   b. eat a lot of cheese

   c. play baseball with friends

4. A **moderate** would want _____ in the government.

   a. no change

   b. some change

   c. many changes

Word Study: The Suffix *-ment*

When the suffix *-ment* is added to a verb such as *enlighten*, it does two things:

- First, it changes the word to a noun: *enlightenment*.
- Second, the word now names a state of being.

Most of the time, you will drop the final *-e* before adding the suffix *-ment*.

enlighten (v.) to inform, to give knowledge
enlightenment (n.) the state of gaining knowledge

Add the suffix *-ment* to the verbs below. Write a definition for each new word. Use a dictionary to check your spelling and definitions.

	+ *-ment*	Definition
1. **judge**		
2. **acknowledge**		
3. **encourage**		
4. **enhance**		

Vocabulary: World History, SV 9781419035029

Name _____   Date _____

The Language of Testing

How would you answer a question like this on a test?

(**Which of the following**) is an example of treason?

    (A) stealing from the grocery store
    (B) lying to your mother or father
    (C) selling your government's secrets
    (D) cheating on a driver's license test

Tip

If you see the words *which of the following* on a test, you have to choose one of the answers (A, B, C, or D) to answer the question.

Test Strategy: If a question has the phrase *which of the following* in it, you may want to ask the question in a different way. Start your restated question with *who, where,* or *what.*

1. How could you say the question above in a different way?

_____

_____

Try the strategy again by asking these questions in a different way.

2. Which of the following is true of royalists?

    (A) They are powerful rulers.
    (B) They support kings and queens.
    (C) They resist change.
    (D) They are kings and queens.

3. Which of the following people might be called conservative?

    (A) a man who always wears the same suit
    (B) a woman who travels to new places every year
    (C) a college student who attends three different schools
    (D) a person who has had many jobs

_____   _____

_____   _____

_____   _____

_____   _____

Name _____   Date _____

On Your Own

Answer the questions.

1. What are you **conservative** about? _____

_____

2. When do people perform **counterrevolutionary** acts? _____

_____

3. How might **enlightenment** lead to a revolution? _____

_____

4. What are you **moderate** about? _____

_____

5. What is the most **radical** idea you've had? _____

_____

6. What things are you **reactionary** about? _____

_____

7. What things might a **royalist** believe? _____

_____

8. What would you consider **treason**? _____

_____

Write On!

You are a French citizen at the time of the French Revolution. On another sheet of paper, write a speech in which you use four promises to try to persuade the public to be either for or against the revolution. Use at least four words from the lesson correctly in your speech.

characterize	**contradict**	**conservative**	**enlightenment**	**royalist**
moderate	**radical**	**reactionary**	**counterrevolutionary**	**treason**

Vocabulary: World History, SV 9781419035029

Name _____   Date _____

Lesson 9 Assessment

Read the sentences. Look for the best word to complete each sentence. Fill in the circle for the answer you choose. The first one has been done for you.

1. When I understand something that had previously confused me, I have a moment of _____.
   - Ⓐ enlightenment
   - Ⓑ treason
   - Ⓒ reactionary
   - Ⓓ conservative

2. _____ might prefer being ruled by a king or queen.
   - Ⓐ Counterrevolutionaries
   - Ⓑ Moderates
   - Ⓒ Royalists
   - Ⓓ Radicals

3. I would _____ Judy as being quite shy.
   - Ⓐ characterize
   - Ⓑ contradict
   - Ⓒ infer
   - Ⓓ verify

4. A _____ does not like the idea of change in government.
   - Ⓐ traitor
   - Ⓑ radical
   - Ⓒ liberal
   - Ⓓ conservative

5. A _____ has extreme political beliefs.
   - Ⓐ conservative
   - Ⓑ moderate
   - Ⓒ heretic
   - Ⓓ radical

6. A person who commits _____ against the government can be sent to prison.
   - Ⓐ enlightenment
   - Ⓑ treason
   - Ⓒ counterrevolutionary
   - Ⓓ reactionary

7. The Congress of Vienna was _____.
   - Ⓐ conservative
   - Ⓑ radical
   - Ⓒ moderate
   - Ⓓ counterrevolutionary

8. The politicians' statements _____ each other.
   - Ⓐ characterized
   - Ⓑ enlightened
   - Ⓒ contradicted
   - Ⓓ moderated

9. A _____ would want to return to the time before a revolution.
   - Ⓐ reactionary
   - Ⓑ moderate
   - Ⓒ conservative
   - Ⓓ treason

10. A _____ does not have extreme political beliefs.
    - Ⓐ radical
    - Ⓑ counterrevolutionary
    - Ⓒ moderate
    - Ⓓ royalist

Name _____ Date _____

Industrialization and Economics

Read the passage below. Think about the meanings of the words in **bold**. Circle any words that end with *-ation*. Remember that *-ation* names a process. Write what you think each circled word means near it in the passage. The first one has been done for you.

The Industrial Revolution

Vocabulary Strategy

Use familiar suffixes to help you understand the meaning of new words.

become more industrial →

The Industrial Revolution began in England during the 1700s. It is characterized by a change from making goods by hand at home to making goods by machines in factories.

The growth of factories brought about new processes as well. One new process was (industrialization,) the development of many new industries that used machines. Some of the new industries made cloth, steel, and trains. Because of industrialization, people moved to cities to work in factories.

Mechanization was another new process. Mechanization means that work is done by machines. If we

tried to **compile**, or put together, a list of machine-made products, the list would be very, very long. Sewing, for example, was now done by machine instead of by hand.

The Industrial Revolution also brought about changes in business. After 1860, **corporations** were started as a new way to own businesses. A corporation is a business in which many people own shares, or part of the company. Some corporations became **monopolies**. A monopoly controls all production and sales for a product. The monopoly in the U.S. steel industry controlled everything that involved steel for a number of years.

New World History Words

corporation

  noun   a large business or company

industrialization

  noun   the development of many factories

mechanization

  noun   the process of using machines to do more tasks

monopoly

  noun   complete control of products or services by a company, person, or state

Now read the passage and practice the strategy again. Circle any words that end in *-ism*. Remember that *-ism* names a belief or a system. Write near each circled word what you think it means.

Economic Changes

The ideas of **capitalism** became important during the Industrial Revolution. Capitalism means people own their own businesses and keep the profits they earn. Business owners decide for themselves what they want to produce.

Industry growth sometimes caused **depressions**, periods in which business activity is very slow, causing many people to lose jobs and become poor.

Some people **critiqued**, or criticized, capitalism and said it allowed business owners to become rich while their workers were poor. Some people thought that **socialism** was better. Socialism is a system in which the government controls businesses and industries and all people are treated equally.

In 1848, Karl Marx wrote a book about **communism**. Under communism, the government owns land and businesses, and makes all of the decisions. Communist governments allow people very little freedom.

More New World History Words

capitalism

   noun   system in which property, business, and industry are privately owned

communism

   noun   a system in which the government controls all businesses and decides what factories and farmers will produce

depression

   noun   a time of little economic activity, or a period of unemployment and poverty

socialism

   noun   a system in which the government controls businesses and industries and all people are treated equally

"I love my **monopoly**. I control every steel **corporation**!"

Other Useful Words

compile

   verb   to put together

critique

   verb   to criticize or judge

Apply the Strategy

Look at a chapter in your textbook that your teacher identifies. Use prefixes and suffixes to help you figure out the meaning of new words.

Name _____ Date _____

 Matching

Finish the sentences in Group A with words from Group B.

Group A

1. Many people work for a _____ that makes computers.

2. Miguel put together, or _____, a list of family and friends to invite to his graduation party.

3. The economic system that allows people to own their own businesses and keep the profits is _____.

4. The development of many new industries starting in the 1700s was called _____.

5. A business that has complete control over sales and production of a product is a _____.

Group B

A. capitalism
B. corporation
C. industrialization
D. monopoly
E. compiled

Group A

6. During the _____ of the 1930s, many people lost all their money on the stock market.

7. Nothing is considered personal property in the system of _____.

8. Government ownership of business and the use of profits for the good of the people is called _____.

9. The use of machines to do work that had been done by hand is _____.

10. When you examine, judge, and criticize something, you _____ it.

Group B

F. communism
G. depression
H. mechanization
I. critique
J. socialism

Name _____ Date _____

Word Challenge: Would You Rather . . .

Read the questions below, think of a response, and write it on the line. Explain your answers. The first one has been done for you.

1. Would you rather **compile** or **critique** recipes for a class cookbook? *I would like to critique recipes because I am a good cook.*

2. Would you rather live during a **depression** or the early days of **industrialization**?

   _____

3. Would you rather live without **mechanization** or **corporations**? _____

   _____

4. Would you rather live under the system of **socialism** or **capitalism**? _____

   _____

Word Challenge: Correct or Incorrect

Write **C** if the sentence is correct. Write **I** if it is not. Rewrite the incorrect sentences. The first one has been done for you.

1. ___I___ **Industrialization** means to make products at home by hand.

   Industrialization means the development of new industries that use machines.

2. _____ People buy shares in a **corporation**.

   _____

3. _____ **Capitalism** is a system that allows private ownership of businesses.

   _____

4. _____ The government owns businesses and uses profits for the good of the people under **socialism**.

   _____

Name _____ Date _____

Extend the Meaning

Write the letter of the word or phrase that best completes each sentence.

1. _____ during a **depression**.
   a. People become wealthy
   b. People lose jobs
   c. More people travel

2. **Industrialization** would cause the development of _____.
   a. many jobs that can be done in school
   b. many new farms
   c. new industries that use machines

3. You might wish to **compile** _____.
   a. information from three books for a report
   b. a warm pair of winter boots
   c. a new baseball hat

4. You can **critique** _____.
   a. a new book or TV show
   b. the ocean
   c. a rainy afternoon

Word Study: The Suffix *-ization*

When the suffix *-ization* is added to an adjective, it does two things:
- First, it changes the adjective to a noun: *industrialization*.
- Second, it changes the word's meaning. The word now names a process or result of something.

industrial (adj.) relating to industries or business
industrialization (n.) the process of developing many industries or businesses

Underline the root word in each *-ization* word. Write a definition of each root word.

1. industrialization _____

2. civilization _____

3. metropolitanization _____

4. socialization _____

Name _____   Date _____

The Language of Testing

How would you answer a question like this on a test?

Each of the following statements is true (except)

- Ⓐ Capitalism involves private ownership.
- Ⓑ Communism involves ownership by the community.
- Ⓒ Socialism involves ownership by socialites.
- Ⓓ A monopoly involves complete control of something.

Tip

The word *except* means you should look for something that means the opposite of the word or phrase before *except*. The opposite of true is false. So in this question, you should look for the answer that is false.

Test Strategy: Make sure you understand the question. Read it carefully. Then, if it has the word *except* in it, ask the question in a different way. Remember that you are looking for the statement that is false.

1. How could you say the question above in a different way?

_____

_____

Try the strategy again by asking these questions in a different way.

2. All of these are corporations except

- Ⓐ a small flower store
- Ⓑ a multimillion-dollar oil company
- Ⓒ an ice-cream maker with stores in every state
- Ⓓ a chain of bookstores

3. All of these are generally results of a depression except

- Ⓐ unemployment
- Ⓑ poverty
- Ⓒ loss
- Ⓓ new jobs

_____

_____

_____

_____

_____

Lesson 10: Industrialization and Economics
Vocabulary: World History, SV 9781419035029

Name _____ Date _____

Answer the questions.

1. What are some features of **capitalism**? _____

_____

2. How is **communism** different from capitalism? _____

_____

3. Would you like to work for a **corporation**? Explain. _____

_____

4. What can cause a **depression**? _____

_____

5. What are some results of **industrialization**? _____

_____

6. What are some of the effects of **mechanization**? _____

_____

7. What would you like to have a **monopoly** on? _____

_____

8. What makes **socialism** different from capitalism? _____

_____

Write On!

You are a political candidate in the mid-1800s. Decide whether you are for capitalism or socialism, and write a paragraph on another sheet of paper describing your political views. Be sure to include at least four good supporting details and use four or more words from the lesson correctly.

capitalism	mechanization	communism	compile	critique
depression	industrialization	corporation	monopoly	socialism

Vocabulary: World History, SV 9781419035029

Lesson 10 Assessment

Read the sentences. Look for the best word to complete each sentence. Fill in the circle for the answer you choose. The first one has been done for you.

1. Unemployment levels rise during a _____.
   - Ⓐ corporation
   - Ⓑ monopoly
   - **Ⓒ** depression
   - Ⓓ capitalization

2. The system that has total government ownership of land and business is _____.
   - Ⓐ socialism
   - Ⓑ capitalism
   - Ⓒ communism
   - Ⓓ industrialization

3. A _____ is bad for consumers because there is no competition in pricing.
   - Ⓐ monopoly
   - Ⓑ socialism
   - Ⓒ capitalism
   - Ⓓ communism

4. The teacher _____ a list of everyone who was absent.
   - Ⓐ contradicted
   - Ⓑ compiled
   - Ⓒ critiqued
   - Ⓓ characterized

5. _____ has made it easier for us to do many things, such as cleaning, cooking, and traveling.
   - Ⓐ Socialism
   - Ⓑ Capitalism
   - Ⓒ Industrialization
   - Ⓓ Mechanization

6. Some people believe that government regulation of certain industries is a form of _____.
   - Ⓐ monopoly
   - Ⓑ socialism
   - Ⓒ capitalism
   - Ⓓ industrialization

7. Even though he has no acting experience, Rodney decided to _____ my performance in the school play.
   - Ⓐ articulate
   - Ⓑ critique
   - Ⓒ infer
   - Ⓓ compile

8. The U.S. economy is built on a foundation of _____.
   - Ⓐ communism
   - Ⓑ monopolies
   - Ⓒ capitalism
   - Ⓓ socialism

9. Many _____ offer stock options to their employees.
   - Ⓐ corporations
   - Ⓑ monopolies
   - Ⓒ depressions
   - Ⓓ mechanizations

10. For a long time, _____ was a characteristic of western civilization, but now many countries in the East are running successful factories and manufacturing goods.
    - Ⓐ communism
    - Ⓑ capitalism
    - Ⓒ socialism
    - Ⓓ industrialization

Social Issues and Reform

Read the passage below. Think about the meanings of the words in **bold**. Create associations between familiar words and ideas and the new words to help you anchor the meaning of the new words. The first one has been done for you.

Reform for Workers

Vocabulary Strategy

Create associations between familiar words and ideas with the new words to help you "anchor" the meaning of new words. You can use a Word Anchor to help you create associations.

After the Industrial Revolution began, many people became factory workers. People who did factory *work* work were referred to as (labor).

One labor problem in the 1800s was that young children were factory workers. Try to **visualize**, or see a picture in your mind, five-year-old children working in factories. People in England and the United States began working for **reform**, or improvements, in factories to solve this problem.

In the United States in the late 1800s, people who worked for reform were called **progressives**. As time passed, the progressives passed new labor laws to help workers.

Workers also helped themselves by starting labor unions. Unions were groups of workers that worked with labor leaders to get better working conditions. Labor leaders told factory owners about the changes they wanted. If factory owners refused to listen to labor leaders, the leaders could start a **strike**. A strike is a decision by labor to stop working in order to get better treatment from factory owners. Strikes can help workers win more money and better working conditions. Another way for people to fight against bad treatment was to stage a rebellion, or **uprising**.

New World History Words

labor
   noun work, or the people working in a factory

progressive
   noun someone who wants to improve society

reform
   noun an improvement in a law, social system, or institution

   verb to improve a law, social system, or institution

strike
   verb to stop working until you get better working conditions or pay

uprising
   noun an act of rebellion, often violent

Name _____ Date _____

Now read the passage below and practice the strategy again. Write near the new words any associations you have that will help you anchor their meaning.

Other Changes and Reforms

Many people in Europe were very poor. They thought they might have a better life in the United States. At the end of the 1800s, there was a lot of **emigration** from Europe. People left Europe to escape from problems there. Many people moved to the United States.

Immigration, the movement of people to a different country, took place at the end of the 1800s. Because of immigration, millions of people from Europe became U.S. citizens. Immigrants had interesting stories about how they left Europe and moved to the United States. Many older immigrants like to **narrate**, or tell their stories, to their children and grandchildren.

There were also reforms by people who wanted to end slavery. They were part of the antislavery movement. Britain slowly ended slavery in its huge empire. In the United States, an 1865 law ended slavery forever.

In the next century, in England and the U.S., laws were passed that allowed most men to vote. However, women also wanted **suffrage**, or the right to vote. In both countries women worked hard to win suffrage. English women finally won suffrage in 1928. Women in the U.S. won it in 1929.

 More New World History Words

emigration
  noun   leaving one's own country to live in another

immigration
  noun   people coming into another country to live and work

suffrage
  noun   the right to vote for a government or leader

Carmen liked to listen to Papi **narrate** how he **immigrated** to the United States.

 Other Useful Words

narrate
  verb   to tell a story

visualize
  verb   to create a picture of something in one's mind

Apply the Strategy

Look at a chapter in your textbook that your teacher identifies. Create associations to help you anchor the meaning of any new words you find.

Name _____ Date _____

The Right Word

Read each sentence. Look at the word or phrase that is underlined. Write one of the words from the box that means the same thing or almost the same thing as the underlined part of the sentence.

emigrated	labor	progressives	strike	narrate

1. _____ My grandmother likes to <u>tell</u> how she came to the United States.

2. _____ The union workers wanted higher salaries, so they decided to <u>stop working</u>.

3. _____ The <u>people who worked for reform</u> believed young children should not work in factories.

4. _____ We said goodbye to many friends before we <u>moved from our country</u> to the United States.

5. _____ Progressives wanted to make conditions better for all <u>people who worked hard jobs</u>.

suffrage	visualize	reform	immigration	uprising

6. _____ People who are against something might stage an <u>act of rebellion</u>.

7. _____ Many people wanted to <u>improve</u> society by helping more children go to school.

8. _____ Women won <u>the right to vote</u> in the United States in 1929.

9. _____ <u>The movement of people to a new country</u> brought millions of people to the United States.

10. _____ Try to <u>see a picture in your mind of</u> yourself skiing down a tall mountain.

Name _____   Date _____

Word Challenge: What's Your Reason?

Think of a reason for each statement and write it on the line. Write your reasons in complete sentences. The first one has been done for you.

1. Why might someone **emigrate** from their home country? _They might emigrate to_
find jobs.

2. Why might someone become a **progressive**? _____

_____

3. Why might workers go on **strike**? _____

_____

4. Why might a group start an **uprising**? _____

_____

Word Challenge: What's Your Answer?

Read each question and write an answer on the line. Answer the questions in complete sentences. The first one has been done for you.

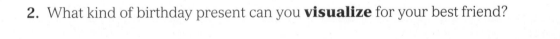

1. What is a reason for **suffrage**? _Everyone should have the right_
to vote on leaders.

2. What kind of birthday present can you **visualize** for your best friend?

_____

3. What kind of **reform** does your school need? _____

_____

4. What kind of **labor** would you not like to do? _____

_____

Lesson 11: Social Issues and Reform
Vocabulary: World History, SV 9781419035029

Name _____ Date _____

Analogies

Use a word from the box to finish each sentence. Write the word on the line.

labor	progressive	reform	uprising

1. Play is to _____ as order is to confusion.

2. Modern is to _____ as traditional is to conservative.

3. Fight is to _____ as disguise is to cover-up.

4. Improve is to _____ as alter is to change.

Word Study: The Suffix *-ive*

When you add the suffix *-ive* to a word, like *progress,* two things happen:
- First, the word changes to an adjective: *progressive.*
- Second, it adds the meaning "tending to" to the word.

Drop the *-e* at the end of some words before adding the suffix *-ive.*

progress (v.) to move
progressive (adj.) tending to move forward

Fill in the chart. Write the new word created by adding the suffix *-ive* and its meaning.

	+ *-ive*	Definition
1. act		
2. create		
3. attract		
4. narrate		

Name _____   Date _____

The Language of Testing

How would you answer a question like this on a test?

Which of the following **compares closely to** the meaning of the word *immigration*?

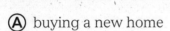

     Ⓐ buying a new home
     Ⓑ taking a short vacation
     Ⓒ leaving one's country
     Ⓓ coming into another country to live

Tip

Compares closely to means is most like.

Test Strategy: If you see the phrase *compares closely to* on a test, rewrite it using the phrase *is most like.*

---

1. How could you say the question above in a different way?

_____

_____

Try the strategy again by asking these questions in a different way.

2. Which of the following compares closely to the meaning of the word *uprising*?

     Ⓐ uplifting
     Ⓑ law
     Ⓒ fight
     Ⓓ improvement

_____

_____

_____

_____

3. Which of the following compares closely to the meaning of *labor*?

     Ⓐ playing tennis
     Ⓑ going for a walk
     Ⓒ digging a ditch
     Ⓓ talking to friends

_____

_____

_____

_____

Name _____ Date _____

 On Your Own

Answer the questions.

1. What can cause someone to **emigrate**? _____

_____

2. How does **immigration** change a country? _____

_____

3. What **labor** do you do every day? _____

_____

4. What things might a **progressive** try to change? _____

_____

5. What would you like to **reform**? _____

_____

6. What might a **strike** accomplish? _____

_____

7. Why is it important for everyone to have **suffrage**? _____

_____

8. What might cause an **uprising**? _____

_____

 Write On!

You are a progressive who is trying to reform the way an industry treats its workers. On another sheet of paper, write a paragraph explaining why you believe reform is necessary. Be sure to include at least four details to support your belief, and use four or more words from the lesson correctly.

emigration	**immigration**	**labor**	**narrate**	**progressive**
reform	**strike**	**suffrage**	**uprising**	**visualize**

Vocabulary: World History, SV 9781419035029

Name _____   Date _____

Lesson 11 Assessment

Read the sentences. Look for the best word to complete each sentence. Fill in the circle for the answer you choose. The first one has been done for you.

1. The airline pilots went on _____ because they felt the number of hours they had to fly was unsafe.
   - Ⓐ strike
   - Ⓑ suffrage
   - Ⓒ uprising
   - Ⓓ reform

2. Since September 11, 2001, the United States _____ policy has grown stricter.
   - Ⓐ immigration
   - Ⓑ progressive
   - Ⓒ labor
   - Ⓓ emigration

3. A _____ would work to provide free healthcare for the poor.
   - Ⓐ labor
   - Ⓑ reform
   - Ⓒ progressive
   - Ⓓ suffrage

4. Dawn was so sure she was going to be nominated homecoming queen that she could _____ the whole experience.
   - Ⓐ strike
   - Ⓑ characterize
   - Ⓒ reform
   - Ⓓ visualize

5. Women did not always have the right to vote in the United States; the Nineteenth Amendment to the Constitution gave women _____.
   - Ⓐ labor
   - Ⓑ suffrage
   - Ⓒ emigration
   - Ⓓ immigration

6. My grandfather loves to _____ stories about his days in the army.
   - Ⓐ narrate
   - Ⓑ strike
   - Ⓒ critique
   - Ⓓ contradict

7. The horrors of the Holocaust led to the _____ of many Jewish families from Europe.
   - Ⓐ immigration
   - Ⓑ uprising
   - Ⓒ suffrage
   - Ⓓ emigration

8. The fire at the Triangle Shirtwaist Factory in 1911 led to a _____ in workplace safety conditions.
   - Ⓐ suffrage
   - Ⓑ progressive
   - Ⓒ reform
   - Ⓓ strike

9. The organization of _____ into unions helped to improve working conditions.
   - Ⓐ suffrage
   - Ⓑ labor
   - Ⓒ progressives
   - Ⓓ reforms

10. Some factory workers took part in violent _____ to revolt against their poor working conditions.
   - Ⓐ progressives
   - Ⓑ suffrage
   - Ⓒ uprisings
   - Ⓓ labor

Vocabulary: World History, SV 9781419035029

Name _____   Date _____

World War I

Read the passage below. Think about the meaning of the words in **bold**. Decide if each new word is a *noun*, *verb*, or *adjective*. In the space above each new word, write *noun*, *verb*, or *adjective*. Use this information to help you figure out what the new word means. The first one has been done for you.

The Beginning of World War I

The war that later came to be called World War I began in Europe in 1914. There were four main causes of the war. Nationalism and imperialism were two causes. The third cause was **militarism**. *noun* The nations in Europe built strong, powerful armies.

The fourth cause was that many countries had formed **alliances**. These were agreements that said all nations in the alliance must fight for each other. One alliance was the Central Powers. Germany was its most important nation. The other alliance was called the Allies. England and France were two of the Allies.

At first the United States did not fight for either side. However, Germany became **belligerent** toward the United States. Germany attacked many U.S. ships.

In 1917, the United States declared war against Germany. The U.S. believed the Allies were fighting to save freedom in Europe. By going to war, the U.S. **restated** its goal of protecting freedom and democracy.

The United States needed soldiers for the war, so Congress passed a **conscription** law. The law required most young men to serve in the army or navy.

Sophia Smith Collection, Smith College

New World History Words

alliance

noun   a partnership among a group of countries

belligerent

adjective   showing anger toward someone or something

noun   person, group, or nation that is at war

conscription

noun   a requirement that able citizens join the military

militarism

noun   a desire to have a strong military

Name _____ Date _____

Now read this passage and practice the vocabulary strategy again. Identify the part of speech of the new words in **bold**. Write the part of speech near the new word.

The End of World War I

In 1917 the United States quickly **mobilized** its army to fight in World War I. To mobilize an army means to prepare soldiers for war and move them where they will fight. U.S. **civilians**, people who are not in the military, also helped during the war. They grew food for the Allies. They also made weapons.

The U.S. government wanted its citizens to believe that it was necessary to fight in World War I. So the government created many **propaganda** posters. Propaganda is information that is used to support a cause. Some propaganda posters encouraged people

to buy war bonds. These posters **implied**, or suggested, that the United States could not win the war without the help of civilians. Bond money helped pay for the war.

The United States helped the Allies defeat Germany and the other Central Powers. On November 11, 1918, German leaders signed an **armistice**, which was an agreement to stop fighting. The world soon had peace again.

"I've been **mobilized** to help with the war effort!"

More New World History Words

armistice

   noun   peace agreement between two fighting countries

civilian

   noun   a person who is not in the military

mobilize

   verb   to take action, or to get ready for war

propaganda

   noun   political information meant to influence people

Apply the Strategy

Look at a chapter in your textbook that your teacher identifies. Identify the parts of speech of new words. Use this information to help you figure out the meaning of new words.

Other Useful Words

imply

   verb   to say something in a way that is not direct

restate

   verb   to say or write something again, in a different way

Name _____ Date _____

 Finish the Paragraphs

Use the words in the boxes to finish each paragraph below. Write the correct words in the blanks. One word in each box will not be used.

belligerent	**conscription**	**militarism**	**armistice**	**alliances**

An important cause of World War I was the building of powerful armies, or

_____, in Europe. Another cause was the growth of agreements
    1.

between nations called _____. The United States joined the fight
    2.

when Germany became _____ and attacked U.S. ships.
    3.

The United States declared war against Germany in 1917. Congress passed a

_____ law that required most young men to serve in the army.
    4.

propaganda	**armistice**	**depression**	**civilians**	**mobilized**	**implied**

In 1917 the United States quickly _____ its army and sent its
    5.

soldiers to Europe. People who were not in the military were called _____.
    6.

The government wanted to convince all U.S. civilians to help win the war, so they

made _____ posters. These posters suggested, or
    7.

_____, that civilians who bought war bonds would help the Allies
    8.

win. In 1918, Germany lost the war and an _____ agreement said all
    9.

fighting would stop.

Vocabulary: World History, SV 9781419035029

Name _____ Date _____

Word Challenge: Correct or Incorrect

Write **C** if the sentence is correct, and write **I** if the sentence is incorrect. Rewrite the incorrect sentences. The first one has been done for you.

1. __C__ The two countries ended the war by signing an **armistice**.

2. _____ When Susan joined the navy, she became a **civilian**.

   _____

3. _____ The government will **mobilize** the troops by sending them into battle.

   _____

4. _____ The poster describing the enemy was government **propaganda**.

   _____

Word Challenge: Finish the Sentence

Read the incomplete sentences below. Write an ending for each. The first one has been done for you.

1. **Conscription** might be unpopular with some people because _they might_
   not want to join the military.

2. I would not become friends with a **belligerent** person because _____

   _____

3. **Militarism** can be a problem because _____

   _____

4. I **restated** what I want for my birthday a few times because _____

   _____

Vocabulary: World History, SV 9781419035029

Name _____   Date _____

Synonyms and Antonyms

Look at each group of words. Circle two words in each group that are synonyms or two words in each group that are antonyms. Then write whether the circled words are synonyms or antonyms on the line below each group.

1. civilian   socialism

   soldier   pharaoh

   _____

2. restate   mobilize

   suffrage   repeat

   _____

3. belligerent   capitalism

   ally   guild

   _____

4. imply   suggest

   labor   strike

   _____

Word Study: The Suffix -ion

When the suffix *-ion* is added to a verb like *conscript*, it does two things:
- First, it changes its part of speech to a noun: *conscription*.
- Second, it changes its meaning to name an action or the result of an action.

conscript (v.) to require someone to join the military
conscription (n.) a requirement that able citizens join the military

A. Underline the root verb and write a definition for each.

1. dedication _____

2. creation _____

3. invention _____

B. Complete the sentence with one of the words from above.

1. I considered my painting of my dog my best _____ so far.

2. The telephone was an _____ of Alexander Graham Bell.

3. It takes great _____ to become a skilled athlete.

Vocabulary: World History, SV 9781419035029

The Language of Testing

How would you answer a question like this on a test?

What is the **main purpose of** propaganda?

- Ⓐ to tell people the truth about politics
- Ⓑ to fool the enemy with lies
- Ⓒ to persuade people to think a certain way
- Ⓓ to get people to join the army

Tip

The word *purpose* can mean *reason* or *use*. The word *main* means that you need to look for the most important purpose.

Test Strategy: If you see a question that uses the word *purpose*, rewrite it using the word *reason* or *use*.

---

1. How could you say the question above in a different way?

_____

_____

Try the strategy again by asking these questions in a different way.

2. What is the main purpose of an armistice?

- Ⓐ to start a war
- Ⓑ to stop fighting
- Ⓒ to improve battle skills
- Ⓓ to enlarge an army

3. For what purpose might a government use conscription?

- Ⓐ to enlarge its military
- Ⓑ to convince people to vote
- Ⓒ to get more money for war
- Ⓓ to build better roads

99

Name _____ Date _____

On Your Own

Answer the questions.

1. What **alliances** do you have in your life? _____
   _____

2. What are the benefits of an **armistice**? _____
   _____

3. Do you have any **belligerents** in your life? _____
   _____

4. What does a **civilian** do? _____
   _____

5. What happens during **conscription**? _____
   _____

6. What are some features of **militarism**? _____
   _____

7. What might you **mobilize** your friends to do? _____
   _____

8. How might you know if something is **propaganda**? _____
   _____

Write On!

You are a member of the U.S. War Department who is in charge of propaganda to promote the war effort during World War I. On another sheet of paper, create a propaganda advertisement that will encourage citizens to buy war bonds, grow food for the troops, and so on. Be sure to include at least three strong, convincing reasons in your advertisement, and use four or more words from the lesson correctly.

alliance	armistice	belligerent	civilian	conscription
imply	militarism	mobilize	propaganda	restate

100
Lesson 12: World War I
Vocabulary: World History, SV 9781419035029

Lesson 12 Assessment

Read the sentences. Look for the best word to complete each sentence. Fill in the circle for the answer you choose. The first one has been done for you.

1. The practice of _____ requires qualified citizens to serve in the military.
   - Ⓐ propaganda
   - 🅑 conscription
   - Ⓒ armistice
   - Ⓓ alliance

2. Uncle Sam became a popular figure seen on U.S. _____ posters during World War I.
   - Ⓐ alliance
   - Ⓑ civilian
   - Ⓒ propaganda
   - Ⓓ armistice

3. England and France formed _____ and fought together during World War I.
   - Ⓐ an alliance
   - Ⓑ an armistice
   - Ⓒ a conscription
   - Ⓓ a propaganda

4. When you _____ something, you expect others to guess what you're thinking.
   - Ⓐ narrate
   - Ⓑ mobilize
   - Ⓒ restate
   - Ⓓ imply

5. A _____ person likes to argue with others.
   - Ⓐ belligerent
   - Ⓑ progressive
   - Ⓒ moderate
   - Ⓓ conservative

6. The unpopular nature of the war _____ people to go out and protest.
   - Ⓐ restated
   - Ⓑ implied
   - Ⓒ mobilized
   - Ⓓ reacted

7. Can you please _____ the question to help us understand it better?
   - Ⓐ imply
   - Ⓑ restate
   - Ⓒ infer
   - Ⓓ compile

8. November 11, the day the Germans signed the _____ to end World War I, is now known as Veterans' Day in the United States.
   - Ⓐ alliance
   - Ⓑ propaganda
   - Ⓒ conscription
   - Ⓓ armistice

9. _____ is practiced by nations that want to use their weapons technology to intimidate other countries.
   - Ⓐ Conscription
   - Ⓑ Armistice
   - Ⓒ Militarism
   - Ⓓ Belligerence

10. Even though she was a _____, Emily helped the war effort by buying Victory Bonds.
    - Ⓐ propaganda
    - Ⓑ civilian
    - Ⓒ belligerent
    - Ⓓ conscription

101

Between the Wars

Read the passage below. Think about the meaning of the words in **bold**. Circle familiar root words that are inside longer new words. Write what you think each word means near it in the passage. The first one has been done for you.

Life Between the Wars

weapon

The peace treaty that ended World War I was signed in 1919. The treaty required **disarmament** by all countries that had fought in the war. Disarmament means a nation makes and owns fewer weapons. The treaty also forced Germany to pay **reparations**, or money for war damages, to the Allies.

Some nations felt that the punishment was unfair. Germany's economy began to suffer. During the 1930s, the economies of other countries weakened, too. Now the Allies needed all the money they could make from trade.

After the war, Britain and France were given mandates, or territories they had to control. Britain and France had to prepare these colonies to rule themselves. Several countries in the Middle East such as Iraq and Syria became mandates.

The 1920s brought wealth and **prosperity** to the United States. People bought cars, radios, and clothing. People hoped that these good years would last forever. Today, we can **evaluate** history and clearly see the causes of the worldwide depression and war to come. In the 1920s, though, only a very few people could see these problems coming.

Vocabulary Strategy

Look for words you know to help unlock the meaning of unfamiliar words in the same family. For example: *consume* can help you unlock the meaning of *consumption*.

New World History Words

disarmament

noun   the act of decreasing the number of weapons a country has

prosperity

noun   wealth or success

reparations

noun   money paid by a losing country to cover damages after a war

Name _____   Date _____

Now read the passage below and practice the vocabulary strategy again. Circle any familiar words inside larger new words that might help you figure out what these words mean.

Hard Times

Many social problems in the United States have been blamed on the **Prohibition** era. Prohibition lasted from 1919 to 1933 when the sale of alcoholic beverages was against the law.

This was also the time of economic depressions around the world. In 1929, the Great Depression began. The Great Depression could be **distinguished**, or set apart, from other depressions because it was much more severe. One cause of this depression was the lack of **consumption** of products. People were not buying and using many things, so prices dropped. Many farms

and factories went out of business. Millions of people lost their jobs and homes.

At least in part, depressions allowed the ideas of **fascism** to spread in Italy and Germany. Under fascism, a country is ruled by a dictator who has total power. In Germany, the fascists were called Nazis. Their cruel dictator was Adolf Hitler.

Fascists also believed in **totalitarianism**. This means the government has total power over the people. Russia and Japan had totalitarian governments.

More New World History Words

consumption
   noun   buying products and using resources

fascism
   noun   a system in which a strong military leader runs the government

prohibition
   noun   the act of making something popular illegal, or the period of time when alcoholic beverages were illegal in the U.S.

totalitarianism
   noun   a system in which one political party controls everything

Consumption is hard when there is no **prosperity**!

Apply the Strategy

Look at a chapter in your textbook that your teacher identifies. Use familiar root words to help you figure out the meaning of new words.

Other Useful Words

distinguish
   verb   to see or understand the difference between things

evaluate
   verb   to judge the quality of something, or to place a value on it

Find the Word

Write a word from the box next to each clue. Then write the word that is formed by the boxed letters. The word answers the question below.

prohibition totalitarian	fascist reparations	prosperity evaluated	fascism distinguish	disarmament consumption

1. making something illegal   _ _ ☐ _ _ _ _ _ _ _ _

2. a removal of weapons   _ _ _ _ _ _ _ _ _ ☐ _ _

3. buying and using products   _ _ _ _ _ _ _ ☐ _ _ _

4. ruled by a dictator   _ _ _ _ ☐ _ _ _ _ _ _ _

5. money for war damages   ☐ _ _ _ _ _ _ _ _ _ _

6. judged   _ _ _ ☐ _ _ _ _ _

7. a government with total control   _ _ _ _ ☐ _ _ _ _ _ _ _

8. belief held by the Nazis   _ _ _ _ _ ☐ _ _

9. a time of wealth   _ _ _ ☐ _ _ _ _ _ _

10. to tell apart   _ _ _ _ ☐ _ _ _ _ _ _ _

What was the money that Germany paid the Allies called?

_ _ _ _ _ _ _ _ _ _ _ s

Name _____ Date _____

 Word Challenge: Quick Pick

Read the following questions. Write an answer for each on the lines below. Write your answers in complete sentences. The first one has been done for you.

1. What was outlawed during **Prohibition**: guns or alcohol? _Alcohol was outlawed_

   during Prohibition.

2. Would a capitalist government encourage sanctions or **consumption**? _____

   _____

3. Is **fascism** a belief in a powerful state or a powerful population? _____

   _____

4. What would a country be doing during **disarmament**: increasing its military or

   decreasing its weaponry? _____

 Word Challenge: Which Word?

Think of a statement for each word below that gives a clue about its meaning. Write your statement next to the word. The first one has been done for you.

1. **totalitarianism** _"I control people's lives."_____

2. **prosperity** _____

3. **reparations** _____

4. **evaluate** _____

5. **prohibition** _____

Name _____ Date _____

Analogies

Use a word from the box to finish each sentence. Write the word on the line.

totalitarianism	prosperity	disarmament	fascism	consumption

1. Democracy is to president as _____ is to dictator.

2. Depression is to hard times as _____ is to good times.

3. Conservation is to save as _____ is to buy and use.

4. Liberty is to democracy as government control is to _____.

5. Arms are to wartime as _____ is to peacetime.

Word Study: The Prefix *dis-*

When the prefix *dis-* is added to a word, it changes the meaning of the word. The prefix *dis-* has several meanings, but the basic meaning is "opposite of."

arm (v.) to supply with weapons
disarm (n.) to reduce the number of or to do away with weapons

Add the prefix *dis-* to the words below and write a definition for each. Use a dictionary to check your spelling and definitions.

	+ *dis-*	Definition
1. believe		
2. connect		
3. place		
4. respect		

Lesson 13: Between the Wars
Vocabulary: World History, SV 9781419035029

Name _____   Date _____

The Language of Testing

How would you answer a question like this on a test?

What is a **characteristic** of consumption?

    (A) People start savings accounts.

    (B) People mend old clothes and socks.

    (C) People buy many pairs of new shoes.

    (D) People take the bus instead of driving.

Tip

A *characteristic* of a thing is something that it usually has or does.

Test Strategy: If you see a question that uses the word *characteristic*, rewrite it to ask for the thing that is true about the subject of the sentence.

1. How could you say the question above in a different way?

_____

_____

Try the strategy again by asking these questions in a different way.

2. What is a characteristic of totalitarianism?

    (A) one powerful political party

    (B) many political parties with little power

    (C) two political parties with equal power

    (D) two main political parties and several lesser parties

_____

_____

_____

_____

_____

3. What is a characteristic of fascism?

    (A) pride in one's country

    (B) good state benefits

    (C) a powerful voting public

    (D) strong government control

_____

_____

_____

_____

_____

Lesson 13: Between the Wars
Vocabulary: World History, SV 9781419035029

Name _____ Date _____

Answer the questions.

1. How can you increase your **consumption** of healthful foods? _____

_____

2. What happens during **disarmament**? _____

_____

3. How would you **evaluate** your government? _____

_____

4. What are some features of **fascism**? _____

_____

5. What are some **prohibitions** you follow at school? _____

_____

6. What are some signs of **prosperity** in a city? _____

_____

7. What might a group of nations receive **reparations** for? _____

_____

8. What power does a common citizen have under **totalitarianism**? Why? _____

_____

Write On!

You are a member of the committee that is drawing up the peace treaty to end World War I. On another sheet of paper, write a rough draft of the treaty that includes at least four main points. Use four or more words from the lesson correctly.

consumption	disarmament	evaluate	distinguish	fascism
prohibition	prosperity	reparations	totalitarianism	

Name _____ Date _____

Lesson 13 Assessment

Read the sentences. Look for the best word to complete the sentence. Fill in the circle for the answer you choose. The first one has been done for you.

1. The teacher found it hard to _____ between the identical twins in her social studies class.
   - (A) evaluate
   - (B) restate
   - (C) narrate
   - (D) distinguish

2. Germany had to pay millions of dollars in _____ after World War I.
   - (A) evaluation
   - (B) reparations
   - (C) disarmament
   - (D) prosperity

3. The Nazi party of Germany believed in _____ and therefore had total control over people's lives.
   - (A) totalitarianism
   - (B) prohibition
   - (C) disarmament
   - (D) consumption

4. _____ of products and resources is a big part of the U.S. economy.
   - (A) Prosperity
   - (B) Prohibition
   - (C) Consumption
   - (D) Totalitarianism

5. Adolf Hitler and Benito Mussolini were two dictators who believed in _____.
   - (A) consumption
   - (B) fascism
   - (C) disarmament
   - (D) prohibition

6. The peace treaty required _____ as a means of preventing future wars.
   - (A) prohibition
   - (B) fascism
   - (C) prosperity
   - (D) disarmament

7. During _____ people in the United States couldn't legally purchase alcohol.
   - (A) Disarmament
   - (B) Fascism
   - (C) Prohibition
   - (D) Consumption

8. Both sides _____ the peace treaty before signing it.
   - (A) evaluated
   - (B) distinguished
   - (C) predicted
   - (D) refuted

9. Jobs are plentiful in times of _____.
   - (A) prosperity
   - (B) evaluation
   - (C) consumption
   - (D) prohibition

10. _____ are often demanded of a country that has lost a war.
   - (A) Prosperity
   - (B) Fascism
   - (C) Reparations
   - (D) Totalitarianism

Name _____   Date _____

World War II

Read the passage below. Think about the meanings of the new words in **bold**. Underline any definitions that might help you figure out what the new words mean. The first one has been done for you.

The Early Years of World War II

World War II began in 1939. Germany's dictator, Adolf Hitler, ordered the **invasion**, or <u>attack</u>, of Poland. Then Britain and France went to war against Germany. Hitler quickly conquered Poland, France, and many countries in Europe. Only Britain remained free to fight Hitler. During this time, Japan conquered countries in Asia.

In 1939 the United States wanted **neutrality**. This means it would not fight for either side. But on December 7, 1941, Japan attacked Pearl Harbor. This U.S. naval base was in Hawaii. Thousands of U.S. citizens were killed. The United States quickly went to war against Japan, Germany, and Italy.

U.S. leaders **assessed**, or carefully guessed, the number of soldiers and weapons they needed

for the war. The leaders also knew there was not enough food to feed both civilians at home and soldiers in Europe and Asia. Therefore, people in the United States received **rations**, or limited amounts of certain foods, such as sugar and meat. Non-food items, like things made of silk and rubber, were also rationed.

The United States planned to win **liberation**, or freedom, for the conquered countries in Europe and Asia.

Vocabulary Strategy

Look for definitions in the text to help you figure out the meanings of new words.

New World History Words

invasion

noun   an attack on a country

liberation

noun   freedom from the control of another country or group

neutrality

noun   refusing to choose a side or express a preference

ration

noun   a limited amount of something

verb   to limit the amount of something

Vocabulary: World History, SV 9781419035029

Name _____   Date _____

Now read the passage below and practice the vocabulary strategy again. Underline any definitions in the text that might help you figure out what the words in **bold** mean.

The End of World War II

From 1941 to 1945, the United States fought with the Allies against Germany and Italy. They fought against Japan in Asia. The Allies helped many countries become free, including France.

Adolf Hitler planned the **genocide** of Europe's Jewish people. Genocide is the killing of an entire group of people. Hitler spread hatred and lies against the Jews throughout Europe. In addition, he had huge death camps built. By the end of World War II, six million Jews had been killed in the death camps.

Communists, socialists, and Roma, or Gypsies, were also killed in these camps. The killing of six million Jews and members of other groups during World War II is called the **Holocaust**.

World War II ended in 1945. Then the Allies began the **occupation** of Germany. Occupation means the control of a defeated nation by the winning nation. U.S. soldiers also occupied Japan. The **demilitarization** of Japan took place, too. Japan could not have an army or own war weapons.

More New World History Words

blockade
  noun   a barrier that prevents supplies from getting into a country

demilitarization
  noun   the act of removing military forces from an area

genocide
  noun   the planned murder of an entire race

Holocaust
  noun   the planned murder of over six million Jews and members of other certain groups in Europe during WWII

occupation
  noun   the act of capturing a country by force, or a job or profession

Other Useful Words

assess
  verb   to figure out the amount of something, or to figure out the truth of a situation

plagiarize
  verb   to claim someone else's ideas or work as your own

Apply the Strategy

Look at a chapter in your textbook that your teacher identifies. Use definitions in the text to help you figure out the meanings of new words you find.

Name _____ Date _____

 Finish the Sentences

Use a word from the box to finish each sentence. Write the correct word on the line.

invasion	assess	rations	genocide	neutrality

1. World War II began with the German attack, or _____, of Poland.

2. In 1939 the United States did not fight for either side because its policy was

   _____.

3. The mass murder of an entire people is _____.

4. Limited amounts of food that people were allowed to buy during the war were called

   _____.

5. The United States had to guess, or _____, how many soldiers it

   would need to fight in World War II.

liberation	Holocaust	occupation	demilitarization	plagiarize

6. If you _____ a story, you are copying it instead of creating it

   yourself.

7. The killing of six million Jews during World War II was the _____.

8. When Germany was defeated, _____ and freedom came to

   countries that had been captured.

9. The United States and three other countries controlled Germany after the war during a

   period called the _____ of that country.

10. After the war, Japan could not have an army due to a policy of _____.

Name _____ Date _____

Word Challenge: Word Association

Read the groups of words below. Write the word from the lesson that best goes with each group. The first one has been done for you.

1. _____blockade_____ barrier, wall

2. _____ not taking sides, no preference

3. _____ release, freedom

4. _____ job, profession, taking control of a country

5. _____ steal ideas, copy, cheat

Word Challenge: What's Your Reason?

Read each question below and write an answer on the line. Answer the questions in complete sentences. The first one has been done for you.

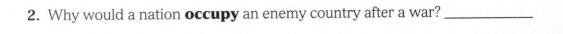

1. Why do librarians need to **assess** the books in the library? ___Librarians___
_____need to know whether there are enough books in good shape.____

2. Why would a nation **occupy** an enemy country after a war? _____
_____

3. Why a might a nation maintain **neutrality** during a war? _____
_____

4. Why should students learn about the **Holocaust**? _____
_____

5. Why are there **rations** for food during a war? _____
_____

Vocabulary: World History, SV 9781419035029

Synonyms and Antonyms

Look at each group of words. Circle two words in each group that are synonyms or two words in each group that are antonyms. Then write whether the circled words are synonyms or antonyms on the line below each group.

1. invasion   attack

   archaeology   feudalism

   _____

3. occupation   plagiarize

   neutrality   copy

   _____

2. liberation   reform

   capture   corporation

   _____

4. ration   peasant

   empire   allowance

   _____

Word Study: The Suffix -ation

When the suffix -ation is added to a verb such as occupy, it does two things:

- First, it changes the verb to a noun: occupation.
- Second, it changes the word's meaning. The word now names the process or result of something.

Drop the -e from the end of a word before adding -ation.

occupy (v.) to take control of something by force
occupation (n.) the act of capturing a country by force

Add the suffix -ation to each root verb to make a new word. Write a definition for each one. Use a dictionary to check your spelling and definitions.

	+ -ation	Definition
1. confirm		
2. adapt		
3. reserve		
4. reform		

114

The Language of Testing

How would you answer a question like this on a test?

Each of the following statements is true

(except)

- Ⓐ Genocide is racially based murder.
- Ⓑ An invasion is an attack on a country.
- Ⓒ Neutrality is capturing a country by force.
- Ⓓ An occupation is a profession.

Tip

The word *except* means you should look for something that means the opposite of the word or phrase before *except*. The opposite of true is false. So in this question, you should look for the answer that is false.

Test Strategy: Make sure you understand the question. Read it carefully. Then, if it has the word *except* in it, ask the question in a different way. Remember that you are looking for the statement that is false.

1. How could you say the question above in a different way?

   _____

   _____

Try the strategy again by asking these questions in a different way.

2. All of these are acts of war except

   - Ⓐ invasion.
   - Ⓑ occupation.
   - Ⓒ genocide.
   - Ⓓ ration.

   _____

   _____

   _____

   _____

   _____

3. All of these signs might be seen at a blockade except

   - Ⓐ Do not enter.
   - Ⓑ No departure.
   - Ⓒ Stop!
   - Ⓓ Welcome.

   _____

   _____

   _____

   _____

   _____

Name _____ Date _____

On Your Own

Answer the questions.

1. Where would you like to have a **blockade**? Why? _____

_____

2. What are the benefits of **demilitarization**? _____

_____

3. What happened during the **Holocaust**? _____

_____

4. What are some of the effects of an **invasion**? _____

_____

5. How might someone respond to **liberation** from a bad situation? _____

_____

6. What do you show **neutrality** toward? _____

_____

7. What are some of the possible effects of a military **occupation**? _____

_____

8. What might you **ration** if you were in a bad situation? _____

_____

Write On!

You are a World War II soldier stationed in Europe. On another sheet of paper, write a letter to your family back home in which you describe your experiences. Include at least four specific details to add to your description. Be sure to use four or more words from the lesson correctly in your letter.

assess	**blockade**	**neutrality**	**genocide**	**plagiarize**	**Holocaust**
invasion	**ration**	**liberation**	**demilitarization**	**occupation**	

Vocabulary: World History, SV 9781419035029

Lesson 14 Assessment

Read the sentences. Look for the best word to complete each sentence. Fill in the circle for the answer you choose. The first one has been done for you.

1. The Holocaust was a massive _____ of Europe's Jewish people.
   - (A) occupation
   - **(B) genocide**
   - (C) blockade
   - (D) invasion

2. After World War II, the Allies began the _____ of Germany.
   - (A) liberation
   - (B) genocide
   - (C) occupation
   - (D) ration

3. After _____ the situation in 1941, the United States decided to send over 16 million soldiers to Europe and the South Pacific.
   - (A) distinguishing
   - (B) plagiarizing
   - (C) conscription
   - (D) assessing

4. The Allies' _____ of the countries occupied by Nazi Germany took place after years of hard fighting.
   - (A) genocide
   - (B) liberation
   - (C) occupation
   - (D) invasion

5. The _____ of Berlin was an attempt by the Soviet Union to limit French, British, and American access to the city.
   - (A) blockade
   - (B) demilitarization
   - (C) ration
   - (D) neutrality

6. The _____ of Japan prevented it from having an army after World War II.
   - (A) plagiarization
   - (B) demilitarization
   - (C) ration
   - (D) blockade

7. Gasoline, rubber, sugar, and butter were given out in _____ to U.S. citizens during World War II.
   - (A) rations
   - (B) blockades
   - (C) occupations
   - (D) neutrality

8. Ed was suspended from school because he had _____ someone else's term paper.
   - (A) assessed
   - (B) occupied
   - (C) plagiarized
   - (D) rationed

9. The German _____ of Poland marked the beginning of World War II.
   - (A) demilitarization
   - (B) blockade
   - (C) occupation
   - (D) invasion

10. The country of Switzerland maintained its _____ and did not get involved in World War II.
    - (A) rations
    - (B) neutrality
    - (C) liberation
    - (D) demilitarization

The World Today

Name _____ Date _____

Read the passage below. Think about the meanings of the new words in **bold**. Underline any examples or descriptions you find that might help you figure out what these words mean. The first one has been done for you.

The Cold War Years

The years between 1945 and 1991 were called the Cold War. During those years, the Soviet Union, now called Russia, was a communist country. During the Cold War, the United States followed a policy called **containment**. It tried to prevent countries from having communist governments. The United States helped rebuild Japan so it would not become a communist country.

After 1945, the United States feared that **nuclear** weapons, weapons with atomic bombs, might be used during a war. The United States and the Soviet Union signed treaties to limit the number of weapons each nation could have.

Britain and other nations in Europe became **welfare** states after 1945. In a welfare state, the government pays for many services that people need. In Britain the government provided everyone with medical care and pensions. However, the government had to **clarify**, or make clear, which services it would provide.

After World War I, many nations experienced **urbanization**. Millions of people moved from towns and farms to cities.

✔ New World History Words

containment

noun   the act of keeping something, such as another country's power, within limits

nuclear

adjective   having to do with weapons that explode by using energy released from splitting atoms

urbanization

noun   a process in which city populations grow and rural areas shrink

welfare

noun   person's health or comfort, or money paid by the government to unemployed, poor, or sick people

Now read this passage and practice the vocabulary strategy again. Underline any examples and descriptions in the passage. Draw an arrow from each to the word it describes.

After the Cold War

When communism ended in the Soviet Union in 1989, many people thought this would bring world peace. Instead, countries used economic **sanctions**, such as boycotts, to punish enemies. When sanctions make goods hard to get, people suffer from the **inflation** of prices on the things they need.

Not every country or group is powerful enough to fight a war or apply sanctions. These groups rely on **terrorism** to **protest** things they want to change. Like inflation, terrorism hurts civilians. However, it is much more dangerous. Nobody knows when or where terrorists will attack.

Some terrorists' actions are very large and well planned. On September 11, 2001, terrorists crashed airplanes into the World Trade Center towers and the Pentagon in the United States. Passengers on another plane fought the terrorists, causing their plane to crash in a Pennsylvania field. Nearly 3,000 people died in these attacks. The **international** community supported the U.S. with donations of money and goods. For example, one very poor Masai tribe in Africa presented a gift of 14 cows to the U.S.

More New World History Words

inflation
  noun   an increase in price of goods

international
  adjective   involving different countries

protest
  verb   to take action against something
  noun   an action taken against something

sanctions
  noun   actions taken against a country that has broken international laws

terrorism
  noun   acts of violence against civilians

Chris found a good use for **inflation**.

Apply the Strategy

Look at a chapter in your textbook that your teacher identifies. Use explanations, descriptions, and pictures to help you figure out the meaning of any new words you find.

Other Useful Words

clarify
  verb   to make something easier to understand

synthesize
  verb   to combine information from many sources

www.harcourtschoolsupply.com
119
Lesson 15: The World Today
Vocabulary: World History, SV 9781419035029

Name _____ Date _____

 Matching

Finish the sentences in Group A with words from Group B. Write the letter of the word on the line.

Group A

1. The U.S. policy to stop the spread of communism was called _____.

2. Dangerous weapons that contain atomic bombs are _____ weapons.

3. When you try to make facts clear and easy to understand, you _____ the facts.

4. When many people move to cities and the cities grow larger, there is _____.

5. When a government provides services like health care, the country becomes a _____ state.

Group B

A. nuclear
B. urbanization
C. welfare
D. containment
E. clarify

Group A

6. _____ means something that happens between two or more nations.

7. An increase in the price of goods is _____.

8. When you combine different facts into one report, you _____ information.

9. We went to _____ the building of a new mall on the swamp.

10. The use of violence against civilians is called _____.

Group B

F. synthesize
G. international
H. terrorism
I. protest
J. inflation

Lesson 15: The World Today
Vocabulary: World History, SV 9781419035029

Name _____   Date _____

 Word Challenge: Correct or Incorrect

Write **C** if the sentence is correct, and write **I** if the sentence is incorrect. Rewrite the incorrect sentences. The first one has been done for you.

1. __C__ Because of **inflation,** we had to cut back on our spending.

2. _____ You need a passport for **international** travel.

   _____

3. _____ We **protested** the new bookstore by buying all our books there.

   _____

4. _____ **Urbanization** takes place in large urban areas.

   _____

 Word Challenge: Quick Pick

Read each question. Decide on the best answer. Explain your answer. The first one has been done for you.

1. Does **urbanization** mean the growth of farms or the growth of cities?

   Urbanization means that people move away from farming areas to the cities and cities grow larger.

2. Who might receive **welfare**: a wealthy doctor or a poor father of five?

   _____

3. Does **inflation** mean that food will be cheaper or more expensive?

   _____

4. Does **containment** help or prevent a country from having too much power?

   _____

Vocabulary: World History, SV 9781419035029

Name _____ Date _____

 Analogies

Use a word from the box to finish each sentence.

clarify	synthesize	international	inflation	urbanization

1. National is about one country as _____ is about many countries.

2. Divide is to separate as combine is to _____.

3. Confuse is to mix up as explain is to _____.

4. Loss of jobs is to depression as high prices are to _____.

5. Rural is to country as _____ is to cities.

 Word Study: The Suffixes -or and -er

When you add the suffix -or or -er to a verb like *protest*, you do two things:
- First, you change the word from a verb to a noun: *protestor*.
- Second, you change the meaning of the word. The new word names a person or thing that does a job.

protest (v.) to show openly you are against something
protestor (n.) someone who shows openly that he or she is against something

Circle the -er and the -or words.

The elevator was broken, so Susan was forced to walk up the stairs. When she reached the fourth floor, Susan presented her idea to the patent lawyer. Her invention was a new computer program for illustrators. To help sell her invention, Susan next had a meeting on the fifth floor with a marketing manager. The two of them made a plan for selling her program. She worked with an advertiser and a famous painter to create an advertisement. She had an actor in mind to present her idea to the public. She hoped he would be available.

The Language of Testing

How would you answer a question like this on a test?

(**Identify**) something people would be most likely to protest.

- Ⓐ a new clothing store
- Ⓑ a high school graduation
- Ⓒ a controversial movie
- Ⓓ the birth of a baby

Tip

When you *identify*, you point out or name something. In a test question, *identify* means to *choose* or *pick* the correct answer.

Test Strategy: Make sure you understand the question. Read it carefully. If you see a question that uses the word *identify*, rewrite it using the words *choose* or *pick*.

1. How would you say the question above in a different way?

_____

_____

Try the strategy again by rewriting the questions using the words *choose* or *pick*.

2. Identify the correct definition for the word *inflation*.

- Ⓐ an increase in the number of citizens
- Ⓑ an increase in the cost of goods
- Ⓒ an increase in the number of troops
- Ⓓ an increase in the amount of food

_____

_____

_____

_____

_____

3. Identify someone who would probably *not* receive welfare.

- Ⓐ an unemployed person
- Ⓑ a poor person
- Ⓒ a student on a scholarship
- Ⓓ a sick person

_____

_____

_____

_____

_____

Name _____ Date _____

 On Your Own

Answer the questions.

1. What is the purpose of **containment**? _____
   _____

2. How does **inflation** affect your life? _____
   _____

3. What are some things that can be described as **nuclear**? _____
   _____

4. What would you like to **protest**? _____
   _____

5. How might **sanctions** harm a country? _____
   _____

6. What are some of the effects of **terrorism**? _____
   _____

7. What are some of the problems with **urbanization**? _____
   _____

8. How does **welfare** work? _____
   _____

 Write On!

You are a politician who is running for federal office. What do you feel is the most important issue affecting the world today? On another sheet of paper, write an essay in which you answer this question. Be sure to include four specific details to support your opinion, and use four or more words from the lesson correctly.

clarify	containment	urbanization	nuclear	terrorism	inflation
protest	sanctions	international	welfare	synthesize	

Lesson 15 Assessment

Read the sentences. Look for the best word to complete the sentence. Fill in the circle for the answer you choose. The first one has been done for you.

1. Some U.S. citizens _____ the U.S. attack on Iraq in 2003.
   - (A) synthesized
   - (B) inflated
   - (C) clarified
   - (D) protested

2. Canada is _____ state that pays for the healthcare of its citizens.
   - (A) a welfare
   - (B) a nuclear
   - (C) a protest
   - (D) an inflation

3. The United States hoped to stop the spread of communism through its policy of _____.
   - (A) inflation
   - (B) terrorism
   - (C) containment
   - (D) welfare

4. The growth of cities and their surrounding suburbs is part of the process of _____.
   - (A) containment
   - (B) urbanization
   - (C) welfare
   - (D) inflation

5. The teacher _____ her instructions by rephrasing them.
   - (A) synthesized
   - (B) clarified
   - (C) protested
   - (D) terrorized

6. The United Nations is _____ organization.
   - (A) a nuclear
   - (B) a welfare
   - (C) a protest
   - (D) an international

7. When you _____ all this information, it is clear that there is only one possible solution.
   - (A) plagiarize
   - (B) protest
   - (C) synthesize
   - (D) inflate

8. The events of September 11, 2001, showed that _____ is a threat to even the strongest countries.
   - (A) terrorism
   - (B) inflation
   - (C) welfare
   - (D) containment

9. Along with an increase in the cost of oil, _____ has made gasoline prices rise.
   - (A) containment
   - (B) inflation
   - (C) protests
   - (D) urbanization

10. Many cities get their electricity from _____ power plants.
    - (A) international
    - (B) welfare
    - (C) nuclear
    - (D) containment

Answer Key

page 8
1. migration
2. culture
3. domesticate
4. archaeology
5. artifact
6. nomad
7. prehistoric
Puzzle Answer: remains

page 9
Word Challenge:
Word Associations
1. artifact
2. significance
3. domesticate
4. differentiate
Word Challenge:
Quick Pick
Answers will vary.

page 10
Analogies
1. archaeology
2. domesticate
3. nomad
4. prehistoric
Word Study
A. 1. cultivation, preparation of land to grow crops
  2. domestication, the taming of animals and plant growing for human use
  3. examination, the process of inspecting closely
B. 1. domestication
  2. cultivation

page 11
Answers to restated questions will vary.
Check students' responses.
1. C   2. A   3. C

page 12
Answers will vary.

page 13
1. A   4. A   7. C   10. B
2. B   5. C   8. A
3. B   6. D   9. C

page 16
1. dynasties
2. pharaohs
3. ancient
4. autocracy
5. empire
6. monotheism
7. bureaucracy
8. polytheism

page 17
Word Challenge:
True or False
1. F; An ancient piece of furniture was made a thousand years ago.
2. F; Early Greeks practiced monotheism because they believed in many gods.
3. T
4. T
Word Challenge:
What's Your Answer?
Answers will vary.

page 18
Word Connections
Yes: autocracy, bureaucracy, pharaoh
No: relevant, monotheism, verify
Word Study
Answers will vary.

page 19
Answers to restated questions will vary.
Check students' responses.
1. A   2. D   3. B

page 20
Answers will vary.

page 21
1. B   4. D   7. C   10. A
2. D   5. A   8. B
3. C   6. B   9. D

page 24
1. B   4. C   7. J   10. H
2. A   5. D   8. F
3. E   6. I   9. G

page 25
Answers will vary.

page 26
Synonyms and Antonyms
1. high society, peasantry
2. lose importance, gain importance
3. republic, autocracy
4. tyrant, elected leader
Word Study
1. predictor, a person who says what will happen in the future
2. philosopher, a person who studies ideas
3. emperor, a person who rules an empire
4. cultivator, a person who prepares land to grow crops

page 27
Answers to restated questions will vary.
Check students' responses.
1. C   2. D   3. A

page 28
Answers will vary.

page 29
1. C   4. B   7. B   10. C
2. A   5. D   8. D
3. B   6. C   9. A

page 32
1. feudalism   5. nobility
2. peasant   6. medieval
3. manors   7. chivalry
4. heretics   8. hierarchy

page 33
Answers will vary.

page 34
Extend the Meaning
1. b   2. b   3. b   4. c
Word Study
A. 1. finer, finest
  2. richer, richest
  3. sharper, sharpest
B. 1. three or more things
  2. two things
  3. three or more things

page 35
Answers to restated questions will vary. Check students' responses.
1. A   2. A   3. C

page 36
Answers will vary.

page 37
1. D   4. D   7. C   10. C
2. B   5. A   8. A
3. B   6. C   9. B

page 40
1. guild
2. apprentice
3. conquest
4. crusade
5. theocracy
6. scholar
7. barter
Puzzle answer: disease

page 41
Word Challenge:
Quick Pick
1. Taking over a country is a conquest.
2. A society ruled by a religious figure is a theocracy.
3. A guild is a group of people who do the same job.
4. A library would be of more interest to a scholar.
Word Challenge:
What's Your Answer?
Answers will vary.

page 42
Analogies
1. apprentice
2. theocracy
3. plague
4. barter
Word Study
1. bartering, trading goods for other goods
2. apprenticing, working for no pay to learn a skill
3. reacting, responding in a certain way because of something that has happened
4. rephrasing, saying something in a different way

page 43
Answers to restated questions will vary.
Check students' responses.
1. C   2. A   3. B

page 44
Answers will vary.

page 45
1. B   4. D   7. B   10. D
2. C   5. A   8. B
3. A   6. C   9. C

page 48
Trade: commercialism, commodity, mercantilism, isolationism, tariff
Travel: compass, isolationism, navigation

Vocabulary: World History, SV 9781419035029

page 49
Word Challenge:
Quick Pick
1. It would trade with other countries.
2. A country with closed borders is practicing isolationism.
3. Navigation involves travel.
4. More art would be better evidence of a renaissance.

Word Challenge:
Correct or Incorrect
1. C
2. I; The cyclists used a compass to determine which direction they were going.
3. C   4. C

page 50
Synonyms
1. commodity, product
2. tariff, tax
3. exchange, trade
4. navigation, course-plotting

Word Study
1. isolation, the process of avoiding contact with others
2. imitation, the process of copying another's actions
3. rejection, the process of refuting an offer

page 51
Answers to restated questions will vary.
Check students' responses.
1. A   2. B   3. D

page 52
Answers will vary.

page 53
1. C   4. D   7. D 10. C
2. B   5. A   8. B
3. D   6. C   9. B

page 56
1. reign
2. parliament
3. restoration
4. diplomacy
5. monarchy
6. despotism
7. absolutism
8. sovereign

page 57
Answers will vary.

page 58
Extend the Meaning
1. b   2. b   3. a   4. b

Word Study
1. absolutism, a system in which one ruler has total power over a country
2. feudalism, a system in which people were given land to work on and were protected by people with more power
3. isolationism, a policy of avoiding contact with other countries
4. mercantilism, a policy of building wealth through trade

page 59
Answers to restated questions will vary.
Check students' responses.
1. A   2. B   3. C

page 60
Answers will vary.

page 61
1. B   4. A   7. B 10. A
2. D   5. C   8. C
3. B   6. B   9. D

page 64
1. imperialism
2. colony
3. expansion
4. missionary
5. nationalism
6. territory
7. assimilation
Puzzle answer: enemies

page 65
Answers will vary.

page 66
Synonyms and Antonyms
1. adaptation, tradition
2. territory, empire
3. growth, decrease
4. patriotism, treason
5. competition, collaboration

Word Study
1. vibration, the process of moving back and forth rapidly
2. migration, the process of moving from one place to another
3. vacation, the act of leaving
4. imitation, the act of copying another's actions

page 67
Answers to restated questions will vary.
Check students' responses.
1. B   2. B   3. A

page 68
Answers will vary.

page 69
1. D   4. C   7. D 10. B
2. A   5. B   8. C
3. B   6. A   9. C

page 72
Answers may vary.
Descriptions of Political Beliefs: conservative, radical, royalist, counterrevolutionary, moderate, reactionary
Political and Cultural Beliefs: enlightenment, conservative, radical, royalist, counterrevolutionary, moderate, reactionary
Actions: contradict, treason, characterize

page 73
Answers will vary.

page 74
Extend the Meaning
1. c   2. a   3. a   4. b

Word Study
1. judgment, the state of passing opinions on others
2. acknowledgment, the state of recognizing an act
3. encouragement, the state of inspiring another
4. enhancement, the state of increasing

page 75
Answers to restated questions will vary.
Check students' responses.
1. C   2. B   3. A

page 76
Answers will vary.

page 77
1. A   4. D   7. D 10. C
2. C   5. D   8. C
3. A   6. B   9. A

page 80
1. B   4. C   7. F 10. I
2. E   5. D   8. J
3. A   6. G   9. H

page 81
Word Challenge:
Would You Rather . . .
Answers will vary.
Word Challenge:
Correct or Incorrect
1. I; Industrialization means the development of new industries that use machines.
2. C   3. C   4. C

page 82
Extend the Meaning
1. b   2. c   3. a   4. a
Word Study
1. industrial, relating to industries or business
2. civil, relating to government and organized society
3. metropolitan, relating to large urban centers
4. social, relating to how people associate with one another

page 83
Answers to restated questions will vary.
Check students' responses.
1. C   2. A   3. D

page 84
Answers will vary.

page 85
1. C   4. B   7. B 10. D
2. C   5. D   8. C
3. A   6. B   9. A

page 88
1. narrate
2. strike
3. progressives
4. emigrated
5. labor
6. uprising
7. reform
8. suffrage
9. Immigration
10. visualize

page 89
Answers will vary.

page 90
Analogies
1. labor
2. progressive
3. uprising
4. reform

Word Study
1. active, tending to move
2. creative, tending to produce things through imaginative skill
3. attractive, tending to arouse interest
4. narrative, tending to tell a story

page 91
Answers to restated questions will vary. Check students' responses.
1. D   2. C   3. C

page 92
Answers will vary.

page 93
1. A 4. D 7. D 10. C
2. A 5. B 8. C
3. C 6. A 9. B

page 96
1. militarism
2. alliances
3. belligerent
4. conscription
5. mobilized
6. civilians
7. propaganda
8. implied
9. armistice

page 97
Word Challenge: Correct or Incorrect
1. C
2. I; When Susan left the navy, she became a civilian.
3. C   4. C
Word Challenge: Finish the Sentence
Answers will vary.

page 98
Synonyms and Antonyms
1. civilian, soldier; antonyms
2. restate, repeat; synonyms
3. belligerent, ally; antonyms
4. imply, suggest; synonyms
Word Study
A. 1. dedicate, to set apart for a specific purpose
2. create, to bring into existence
3. invent, to produce something for the first time through imagination

B. 1. creation
2. invention
3. dedication

page 99
Answers to restated questions will vary. Check students' responses.
1. C   2. B   3. A

page 100
Answers will vary.

page 101
1. B 4. D 7. B 10. B
2. C 5. A 8. D
3. A 6. C 9. C

page 104
1. prohibition
2. disarmament
3. consumption
4. fascist
5. reparations
6. evaluated
7. totalitarian
8. fascism
9. prosperity
10. distinguish
Puzzle answer: reparations

page 105
Word Challenge: Quick Pick
1. Alcohol was outlawed during Prohibition.
2. A capitalist government would encourage consumption.
3. Fascism is a belief in a powerful state.
4. During disarmament, a country would be decreasing its weaponry.
Word Challenge: Which Word?
Answers will vary.

page 106
Analogies
1. fascism
2. prosperity
3. consumption
4. totalitarianism
5. disarmament
Word Study
1. disbelieve, to reject belief
2. disconnect, to become detached
3. displace, to remove from the proper place
4. disrespect, to have a lack of respect for

page 107
Answers to restated questions will vary. Check students' responses.
1. C   2. A   3. D

page 108
Answers will vary.

page 109
1. D 4. C 7. C 10. C
2. B 5. B 8. A
3. A 6. D 9. A

page 112
1. invasion
2. neutrality
3. genocide
4. rations
5. assess
6. plagiarize
7. Holocaust
8. liberation
9. occupation
10. demilitarization

page 113
Word Challenge: Word Association
1. blockade
2. neutrality
3. liberation
4. occupation
5. plagiarize
Word Challenge: What's Your Reason?
Answers will vary.

page 114
Synonyms and Antonyms
1. invasion, attack; synonyms
2. liberation, capture; antonyms
3. plagiarize, copy; synonyms
4. ration, allowance; synonyms
Word Study
1. confirmation, the process of giving approval
2. adaptation, the process of making fit for the surroundings
3. reservation, the process of arranging to have something held for one's use
4. reformation, the act of improving a law, social system, or institution

page 115
Answers to restated questions will vary. Check students' responses.
1. C   2. D   3. D

page 116
Answers will vary.

page 117
1. B 4. B 7. A 10. B
2. C 5. A 8. C
3. D 6. B 9. D

page 120
1. D 4. B 7. J 10. H
2. A 5. C 8. F
3. E 6. G 9. I

page 121
Word Challenge: Correct or Incorrect
1. C   2. C
3. I; We protested the new bookstore by refusing to buy our books there.
4. I; Urbanization takes place in rural areas.
Word Challenge: Quick Pick
1. Urbanization means that people move away from farming areas to the cities and cities grow larger.
2. A poor father of five might receive welfare.
3. Inflation means that food will be more expensive.
4. Containment prevents a country from having too much power.

page 122
Analogies
1. international
2. synthesize
3. clarify
4. inflation
5. urbanization
Word Study
elevator, lawyer, computer, illustrators, manager, advertiser, painter, actor

page 123
Answers to restated questions will vary. Check students' responses.
1. C   2. B   3. C

page 124
Answers will vary.

page 125
1. D 4. B 7. C 10. C
2. A 5. B 8. A
3. C 6. D 9. B

Vocabulary: World History, SV 9781419035029